THE ART OF
SOUL - WINNING

by

Murray W. Downey

BAKER BOOK HOUSE
Grand Rapids, Michigan

Copyright © 1957 by
Baker Book House Company

Paperback Edition 1973
ISBN: 0-8010-2820-5
Library of Congress Catalog Card Number: 57-9523

First Printing, March 1957
Second Printing, June 1958
Third Printing, January 1960
Fourth Printing, February 1963
Fifth Printing, October 1964
Sixth Printing, July 1967
Seventh Printing, December 1969
Eighth Printing, December 1972

PHOTOLITHOPRINTED BY CUSHING - MALLOY, INC.
ANN ARBOR, MICHIGAN, UNITED STATES OF AMERICA
1972

FOREWORD

The work of winning souls for Christ is undoubtedly the greatest work that God permits men to do. Soul-winning is, however, rarely accomplished by a general appeal from the the pulpit. General preaching has its place, but ordinarily it is only preliminary to individual soul-winning. The most effective preachers unhesitatingly declare their conviction that individual work is of primary importance and that nothing else is a substitute for it. Henry Ward Beecher, for example, once said, "The longer I live, the more confidence I have in those sermons preached where one man is the minister and one man is the congregation; where there is no question as to what is meant when the preacher says, 'Thou art the man.'"

The first disciples of Jesus were enlisted one at a time. We are not told just how all of the twelve apostles were won to Christ, but the six of whom we do know were won in this way. They were either sought out by Christ Himself or brought to Him by others, as Andrew brought his brother Peter, and Philip brought his friend Nathanael. In the Gospels we so often see Jesus dealing with individuals that we are constrained to think that it must have been with Him a favorite method of work. There is no doubt that the seeking of single individuals by Christians has been the most effective way of winning souls for Christ from the beginning of the Christian church to the present day.

Mr. Downey's book is a clear, Scriptural, and practical presentation of how to be a successful soul-winner by personal work. The material of the book has been used by him for years in his class on soul-winning in the Bible school in which he teaches. In the opening section he deals with the spiritual preparation necessary for effective soul-winning. He brings out very clearly the necessity of a Spirit-filled life for the worker. In the second section he considers the difficulties and objections a Christian worker is likely to encounter as he deals with souls. The third part of the book is really unique in books of this kind. In it he shows how to deal with the adherents of some of the most important cults found in our land. The book will be found extremely helpful for personal or group study or as a text for the classroom. Every page of the book is Scripturally grounded. The questions at the end of each chapter are searching and helpful. The book is replete with practical instruction on the art of soul-winning.

Steven Barabas

PREFACE

Every Christian should shudder at the thought of meeting the Lord of the harvest with no souls, no sheaves to lay at His blessed feet. The Great Commission of our Lord Jesus Christ to go into all the world to preach the gospel to every creature is not a challenge: it is a command. It is a charge to keep. To live in daily disobedience to the Lord and Captain of our salvation, puts a bold question mark after the profession some make of being children of God. According to Bible standards, children of disobedience are children of wrath. That alone should startle some to awaken from their spiritual slumber. The Bridegroom cometh. It is midnight. Get oil in your lamp and *prepare* to meet thy God.

If every student graduated from a Bible School is not imbued with the spirit of evangelism, time, talent and training were invested in vain. If pastors and peoples have no passion for souls, the grace of God has been received in vain. In our churches we have too many shirkers and jerkers and too few worshippers and workers. The deadly philosophy of an easy-believism has such a strangle-hold of even our evangelical churches that there is an urgent need for divine deliverance. Faith without works is twice dead. A more careful study of the epistles of James and John, Paul and Peter, makes one wonder if some of our crossless Christians were ever truly born again. It has been estimated that only five out of every one hundred evangelical Christians make any earnest effort to win souls. To help close this ghastly gap is one objective of this book.

With devilish devotion, Communists conspire to girdle the globe. In less than forty years they have gained the mastery of over one-third of the world. The remaining two-thirds of the areas of earth are dangerously infiltrated with this atheistic philosophy. But in this dark and critical hour, the church can be assured that when the enemy comes in like a flood, the Spirit of the Lord shall lift up a standard against him. God has promised to pour out His Spirit upon *all* flesh in the last days. But God does not pour out His Spirit arbitrarily. God pours out His Spirit upon prepared peoples. Let Christians rally to prepare the way of the Lord. Let the saints make His paths straight. Christ has promised His power and His presence to those who participate in His program to the end of the age. Even the gates of hell *cannot* prevail against the church. The gospel shall be preached in all the world for a witness and then the end of the age shall come. Let Christian soldiers set up their banners and claim victory. God is able to make the church both militant and triumphant.

While many books have been written on evangelism and soul-winning, I do not know of any that could be considered a *comprehensive* text-book, setting forth a suitable *standard* for study and mastery. A student who can pass the examinations at the end of the lessons in this book with a minimum of seventy per cent average, will have prepared himself to meet about every class and condition of men. Though there are cults innumerable, the issues treated in this course, recur so often that the mastery of these will prepare a soul-winner to deal with any false system.

The writer is indebted to the graduating class of 1955 at the Western Canadian Bible Institute in Regina for very valuable assistance given in the preparation of the material on Cults. Primary sources have been carefully checked to make sure that no misrepresentation was made of any doctrine. These have been documented for the benefit of those who might imagine that any injustice has been done to those holding contrary views.

An effort has been made to keep constantly before the student that he is in training for soul-*winning*, not soul-*antagonizing*. The gospel messenger must be full of grace as well as truth. The spiritual life of the soul-winner is basic. A carnal Christian is not fit for this spiritual service. Fortunately, such are usually disinterested in such effort. But sometimes in a gust of enthusiasm, Christians will seek to win souls to Christ when their worldliness and carnality only nauseate the unsaved.

For churches conducting Leadership Training Classes, a companion booklet, *Manual on Soul-Winning*, has been prepared. This short course can be taught in ten class periods. It is an abridgment of lessons taught in this book. The short course is suitable for lay-workers. The twenty lessons of this course are covered in two quarters of twelve weeks each, taking two hours per week per quarter. For schools using the semester system, the course might well occupy two semesters if the section on Cults is used as a springboard for the study of additional cults.

—The Author.

CONTENTS

PART I

PREPARATION FOR SOUL-WINNING

LESSON I

THE IMPORTANCE OF SOUL-WINNING

I. *It helps the Christian.*

The Christian who goes out to win the lost and glows with genuine testimony for his Lord, is invariably one who grows in grace and in the knowledge of his Lord and Saviour Jesus Christ. A barren believer is good for nothing. A Christian is like a tree planted in the earth to reproduce his own kind. As an apple tree produces apples and a pear tree pears, so a Christian should yield Christians. The one who finds Christ and then follows Christ must inevitably become a fisher of men. The fruit of the Spirit is to be distinguished from the fruit of the righteous. The fruit of *right* living is souls. Soul-winning helps the Christian to live right. If he lives right, he will seek the lost, study his Bible, supplicate for their salvation, suffer for righteousness and serve Christ with an eye single to His glory.

MATT 4:19
Matt. 7:19
Ps. 1:3
Prov. 11:30
John 15:16
Mark 1:17

II. *It helps the church.*

The church that is aflame with soul-winning zeal is a progressive church. If worldliness and carnality are allowed to extinguish the fires of evangelism, the church has lost its claim to continuance. Paul reckoned it vain to found churches that did not hold forth the Word of Life in the midst of perverse peoples. The church at Thessalonica was ablaze with holy zeal to take the gospel to others. This was not abnormal. They were simply following the pattern established by Christ for the Jerusalem and Judean churches. Evangelize or fossilize! That is the issue. A church without its lamp lit in this dark world is running the risk of having its lampstand removed. For such criminal negligence, let the church repent and be revived or be removed.

Rev. 3:16
Phil. 2:15-16
I Thess. 1:8

I Thess. 2:14
Acts 1:8
Rev. 2:5
Ezek. 3:17-19

11

III. *It helps the community.*

When a few Christians in a church get truly revived, the whole community will soon benefit from the
blessing. When such a revival came to the island of
Lewis off the northwest coast of Scotland in 1949,
drinking-houses were closed, dance halls went out of
business, scorners and scoffers were transformed into
singing saints and police stations became prayer meeting houses as the foul stench of crime was blown away
by the breath of revival. Corruption in our communities
is due to the fact that our churches have lost their salt
savor. It is wrong to stand afar off from the drunkard
and the derelict, to cast stones of condemnation at them.
We must go to them, woo them, win them, weep over
them. Our commission is to

> Rescue the perishing, care for the dying,
> Snatch them in pity from sin and the grave;
> Weep o'er the erring one, lift up the fallen,
> Tell them of Jesus, the mighty to save.

We must not allow denominational barriers to blur
our vision of winning souls to *Christ*. A Spirit-given
passion for souls will break through all barriers of creed,
class, color and condition. The juvenile and parental
delinquency in our communities is attributable to the
lukewarmness, if not the apostasy, of evangelical churches which are not evangelistic.

IV. *It helps the country.*

It was not Babylon that destroyed Judah in 588 B.C.:
it was backsliding. It was not Assyria that destroyed
Israel in 721 B.C.: it was sin. Those wicked nations
were but the "rod of God's anger" for the chastisement
of God's people who had ceased to be a good testimony
for Him in the midst of the earth. Canada and America
are living under the shadow of impending judgment because we have gone far away from God. Nineveh repented and averted imminent disaster. But Nineveh did
not repent until Jonah repented.

Margin notes:

The Lewis Awakening

1949-53

Duncan Campbell

Pub. by The Faith Mission, Edinburgh,12, Scotland

MATT 5:13

9+10
II Cor. 5:9-14

Jeremiah
Zeph. 1:4-18
Hosea 4:1-6
Isa. 10:5+6

Jonah 3

Jonah 1-2

Jer. 6:6-17

Isa. 28:7

Dan. 5
Hos. 4:11

Isa. 59:19

Although the phenomenal growth of Communism in 38 years from 40,000 to 800,000,000 is enough to make a wide-awake citizen shudder, it will not be Communism that will destroy us. Sin and impenitence are the parents of national disaster. Consider the fact that America spends six times as much on liquor as for all religious and welfare activities and conclude that the writing is on the wall—unless we repent. Just as the evangelistic efforts of the Wesleys and Whitefield saved England from the horrors of revolution, so a revived church in America could turn the tide at this critical hour.

V. *It helps the cause of Christ everywhere.*

Matt. 28:19

Matt. 13:38

II Tim. 2:1
Acts 1:8
Eph. 5:18

If a Christian is taught and trained to be a missionary at home, he will be a worth-while missionary abroad. No Mission Board should gamble on the prospect of a candidate winning souls on the foreign field who has not been winning souls here in the home field. A trip across the ocean blue will not make a missionary true. The field is the world. Prospective missionaries need to give more attention to the *in*fit than they do to the *out*fit. One who is endued with power from on high will be a witness *both* in Jerusalem and Judea as well as unto the uttermost part of the earth.

VI. *It reaches all classes.*

Luke 14:21

John 3:16

John 3
John 4
John 1
John 9

Matt. 9:9
Luke 19:1-10
Luke 23:43

Personal soul-winning is important because it reaches all classes. Whether rich or poor, old or young, small or tall, educated or illiterate, religious or irreligious, moral or immoral, there is some avenue of approach to every sin-sick soul. Christ talked to individuals of all classes. The spiritually bewildered ruler of the Jews, the sinful Samaritan woman, the guileless Nathanael, the unobtrusive Andrew, the man who was dropped from the membership of a Jewish synagogue, Matthew the tax-collector, Zacchaeus the publican, the thief on the cross, were each singled out for counsel and attention. No

John 7:37-39

church should withhold the glorious gospel from any creature. The church is not to be a reservoir but a river that channels out the living waters to a thirsty world.

VII. *It meets all conditions.*

Isa. 55:1

Matt. 11:28

Phil. 3:1-10

Rom. 1:14-16

Personal work in soul-winning is important because it can be done in all conditions of *weather.* A person can stand on the street corner on a stormy night and point a soul to Christ. Under the blistering heat of the African sun or in an icy igloo of the Antarctic, the sweet gospel story can be told by God's ambassador.

It meets all conditions of *workmen,* dentists and doctors, teachers and professors, barbers and brick-layers, carpenters and clothiers, lawyers and laundrymen, athletes and actors, magistrates and masons.

It meets all conditions of *worshippers,* the priest or the preacher, the monk or the nun, the Mormon or the modernist, the Hindu or the Mohammedan, the Christian Scientist or the Unitarian. Wherever, whenever or however men may die, the soul-winner must seek to blockade the broad road to hell and turn sinners anywhere and everywhere to the only Saviour, our Lord Jesus Christ.

VIII. *It conforms to Christ's command.*

John 14:15

Mark 16:15

Luke 6:46

Jas. 4:17

Ezek. 3:17-19

Acts 20:26

II Cor. 5:10

Rev. 3:16

The church has majored on the promises of God and minored on His commands. Disobedience is sin. The Great Commission to go and preach the gospel to every creature is not a challenge: it is a command, a charge given by the *Lord.* Negligence is sin. Our failure to win souls is reprehensible and wicked. The church has failed to take Christ seriously. The blood of millions is on our hands. The unsaved of our generation will witness against us on that day when we have to stand before the tribunal of heaven. To be saved from sin and the flames of an eternal hell carries with it not only unspeakable privileges but frightening responsibilities.

IX. *It produces abundant results.*

John 1:41

Acts 2:41

John 15:8

II Chron. 7:14

Andrew brought his brother Simon to Jesus and Simon Peter won thousands to the Saviour. Kimball led Dwight L. Moody to Christ and Moody won tens of thousands to Jesus. God is glorified in our bearing *much* fruit. Let us attempt great things for God and expect great things from God. Revival in our generation is not only needed. It is imperative.

Examination on Lesson I

Marks	
8	1. In what ways is soul-winning shown to be important?
20	2. Quote Ps. 1:3; Prov. 11:30; John 15:16; Mark 1:17.
10	3. What are your reasons for believing that every Christian should win souls?
10	4. By use of Scripture reference and illustration, prove that apostolic churches were soul-winning churches.
10	5. Why is negligence in soul-winning so reprehensible?
5	6. Illustrate from your own reading or from the notes how revival helps a community.
6	7. From II Cor. 5:9-14, find at least three substantial motives for engaging in soul-winning effort.
5	8. Briefly from the book of Jeremiah, make clear why the Lord had to permit Babylon to remove Judah.
6	9. From what you recall of the passage in Zeph. 1:4-18 and in Hos. 4:1-6, how do you account for the captivity of Judah in 588 B. C. and of Israel in 721 B. C.?
3	10. What three nations went to their doom through drink?
5	11. Discuss the relationship of home missions to foreign missions in the matter of providing personnel.
6	12. Illustrate from the life of Christ how soul-winning reaches all classes.
6	13. Illustrate the importance of soul-winning from the standpoint of meeting all conditions of weather, workmen and worshipers.
35	14. Quote John 14:15; Mark 16:15; Luke 6:46; Jas. 4:17; Rom. 1:14-16.
5	15. Illustrate from the life of Andrew the value of personal soul-winning.
10	16. Does your home church believe that personal soul-winning is very important? Do you? Suggest ways for making an evangelical church evangelistic.

$$150 \times \frac{100}{150} = 100$$

LESSON II

CONDITIONS FOR SUCCESS
IN WINNING SOULS TO CHRIST

I. *A clean heart.*

Ps. 51:10-13

II Cor. 6:17-7:1

II Tim. 2:21

Prov. 28:13

I Cor. 3:16-17

It is more important to be clean than it is to be clever if the Holy Spirit is to use us in winning souls to the Saviour. To be a vessel unto honour and fit for the Master's use, confess and forsake every form of evil, make your heart a happy home for God the Holy Spirit and He will use you to woo and win the lost to their Lord.

I John 1:4

I John 1:7-10

I John 2:1

A holy life is not a sad life. John wrote his epistle in order that the children of God's family may know fulness of joy. But the apostle of love knew that sin was a kill-joy. Therefore he admonished his converts to keep short accounts with God by confessing their sins, claiming divine forgiveness and cleansing, and forsaking the practice of sin. The pure in heart are truly happy and blessed.

Matt. 5:8

Matt. 5:13-14

Matt. 5:11-12

Prov. 4:23

Luke 15:8-10

I John 1:5

Acts 5:1-11

Those of pure heart are indeed the light of the world, the salt of the earth, the ones who can rejoice and be exceeding glad when persecuted for the sake of righteousness. Out of the heart are the issues of life. Let the individual Christian in every church get a broom and do some house-cleaning and the lost coins will be found. Sinners will not be saved and heaven will not rejoice as long as unconfessed sin is allowed to lurk within the lives of God's people. God is Light. When a church is walking in fellowship with God, sin is easily detected and quickly judged.

II. *A consecrated heart.*

Rom. 12:1-2

The redeemed child of God should be so overmastered by the love of Christ that in heart-worship he will gladly present his body a living sacrifice to God the Holy Spirit.

17

II Cor. 5:14
I Cor. 6:19-20

Matt. 22:37

Matt. 22:38

The reason why only an estimated 5 per cent of born-again Christians participate in earnest efforts to win souls, is a heart problem. When Christians fail to love God with all their heart and thus break the first commandment, is it any wonder that they cannot keep the second commandment to love their neighbours as themselves?

A consecrated heart will mean consecrated bodies. Consecrated bodies will not prefer the cushion to the cross. Strong stalwart soldiers of the cross, ready to endure hardness for Jesus' sake, are thinning out in the ranks of some evangelical churches. It is wrong to be conformed to this world; wrong to refuse to present our bodies a living *sacrifice*; wrong to drift in the current of apathy and apostasy and let souls go to hell without a word of warning from us. The church must stop looking for excuses and begin looking for opportunities. Christians, who say in the Winter, "It is too cold," will complain in the Summer, "It is too hot." In the Spring they will be too busy, in the Fall too lazy, and in eternity too late to repent or compensate for their neglect. Check the drift! Change the course! Go against the current! Present your body a *living* sacrifice to God the Holy Spirit. A seed planted in the ground to die, will in dying, multiply itself a hundredfold.

II Tim. 2:3-4

Rom. 12:2

Heb. 2:1-4

II Cor. 5:11

Ecc. 11:1-6

I Kings 20:39-40

Matt. 25:30

Matt. 7:15-20

John 12:24

III. *A compassionate heart.*

Acts 2:1-4

II Cor. 5:14

Gal. 5:22

Rom. 5:5

A clean heart that is consecrated to God is one that the Holy Spirit can fill with His constraining love. Love for souls is not a natural impulse. It is the love of *Christ* that must constrain. The fruit of the *Spirit* is love. If one has to strain to love the lost, he is not being constrained.

Paul was filled with this divine compassion and it made him count not his life dear. Paul was expendable. Paul preached with tears coursing down his cheeks. Paul suffered joyfully because he did not merely pity the lost but he had compassion on them. Some people can pity the poor peoples of heathen lands; they can pity them so

Acts 20:24

Acts 20:31

II Cor. 7:4

Rom. 9:3

much that they will weep when they hear or read about their plight. But the one who has compassion will do something about it. Paul was willing to be accursed of God if only his Jewish brethren could be saved. He went to them even when they were threatening to kill him

Acts 20:22-24

because he had compassion on them.

Heb. 2:14

Paul had the compassion of Christ. Christ's compassion made him willing to face the Goliath of death to redeem us from the tyranny of the mighty prince of this world.

Luke 19:41

Christ wept over the blindness of religious Jerusalem. If there were more tears of compassion in the eyes of God's people on earth, there would be less weeping and

Ps. 126:6

wailing in hell among the damned and the lost. It is

Matt. 25:30

not argument that will win souls: it is compassion. One may have the truth but if it is not spoken with love and

Eph. 4:15

compassion, it is more likely to kill than quicken. One may witness without compassion but he will not win.

Rom. 10:1

IV. *A heart in communion with God.*

Gal. 4:19
Isa. 40:31
Acts 1:14
Acts 2:42
Acts 4:31
Acts 6:4
I Thess. 5:17
Luke 18:1

Paul prayed earnestly for the salvation of souls. He prayed before they were saved: he prayed after they were saved. A prayerless Christian will be a powerless Christian. The phenomenal results in soul-winning in the Acts of the Holy Spirit through the apostles in the New Testament can only be explained by the mighty praying recorded in that book. No one can have tact in dealing with men who does not keep contact with God in prayer, praying without ceasing, praying before you speak to souls, while speaking and after you have spoken. As in physical birth, a mother carries a burden for the birth of her child, so in bringing forth spiritual children, some one will have to accept a God-given burden for the salvation of a soul and be willing to travail in prayer till it is brought forth. When that child is born into the kingdom of God, some prayer warrior will be able to say with Hannah of old, "For this child I prayed

I Sam. 1:27

and the Lord hath given me my petition which I asked of Him."

Any church can have a revival if it can find just a few

Matt. 18:19
Luke 11:1-13

Matt. 6:6
John 15:5

Ezek. 3:17-19

Rev. 3:1

individuals who will get thoroughly right with God and then seek God's face importunately for an outpouring of His Spirit in convicting power upon lost souls. Here is a hidden ministry open to any child of God. Without such service, it is futile to reach, teach or preach to lost souls. When a church stops praying, it stops progressing. A prayerless Christian is so utterly backslidden that he will not care if his dearest friends go to hell unwarned. It is more likely that such a person has only a name to live but is still dead in trespasses and sins.

V. *Spiritual enduement.*

Luke 24:47-49

Acts 1:8

John 16:7-11
Rom. 1:16
John 1:13
Acts 5:3-5

Acts 4:24-33

Acts 6:10

Luke 1:35

John 3:8

John 7:38-39

Zech. 4:6

The supreme condition for success in soul-winning is a specific enduement of power from on high. The evangelization of the world is a colossal task. When the Lord commissioned His disciples to make the gospel known throughout the world, He commanded them to tarry before going forth to teach. They were to tarry *until* they knew they were endued with power from on high. Only the power of God can convict and convert the sinner. God alone can regenerate. God alone can save. But the Holy Spirit is God. The reason why the Roman government, the Jewish Sanhedrin and all the powers of hell could not stop the revival that came to the disciples in that upper room in Jerusalem, was because there was no power or combination of powers on earth that could resist God. God is omnipotent. The Holy Spirit is omnipotent. A man might just as well try to harness the wind or hinder the waters of the mighty Niagara as to stop the moving of the Spirit of God.

VI. *The sword of the Spirit.*

Eph. 6:17

Heb. 4:12

Acts 8:26-38

II Tim. 4:3

No one is well equipped to win souls who does not know how to wield the sword of the Spirit which is the Word of God. The successful soul-winner must study the Word till he knows how to apportion and apply the Word to individual cases. Though we are not the Lord's lawyers but just His witnesses, we are nevertheless ex-

II Tim. 3:16
Tit. 1:11
II Tim. 2:24-26

horted to rebuke, reprove, to shut the mouths of the gainsayers, doing so with all longsuffering and doctrine, with meekness instructing those who oppose themselves in order that they may be recovered from their Satanic snares.

VII. *Some further suggestions.*

1. Do not begin with criticism. Matt. 7:1. No one can hope for success as a fisher of men if he does nothing but stand off and throw stones at the fish.

Luke 19:10

John 20:21

2. Do not begin with condemnation. John 3:17. Jesus did not come into the world to condemn the world. He came to seek and to save the lost. And as the Father has sent the Son, so sends He you.

John 4:20-21

3. Do not argue. II Tim. 2:24-26. The servant of the Lord *must not* strive. He must be gentle unto *all* men. He is not to walk off in disgust when he meets some tempestuous trooper. He is to be patient, apt to teach, meekly instructing those who oppose them, looking to God to recover such from Satan's seductive snares.

Isa. 53:7

Luke 23:9

4. Do not antagonize. Matt. 10:16; Prov. 11:30. Even though the soul-winner often finds himself like a sheep among wolves, he is never to snap and snarl at the sinner. The Christian is to be like Jesus. Sometimes we may witness more effectually by our silence than by our loud speech. Be wise as a serpent. Be harmless as a dove.

5. Begin with honest commendation. John 1:42, 47. Jesus' first comment to Simon (meaning "sand") was that He would make him Cephas (meaning a "stone"). The shifty unstable Simon was to be the strong and stalwart Peter. Look hopefully upon the sinner. Look upon

Heb. 7:25

Rom. 1:16

him in the light of what Christ can do for him. Believe in your God and in your gospel.

6. Find out a man's temporal interests before opening the subject of eternal interest. Luke 5:1-11. Business had taken a deep sag. The fishermen were discouraged. They were not quite in the mood for a religious talk. Jesus took an interest in their business. He had a suggestion to make which was followed and business began

to boom. Their interest was won. The way was now open to deal with eternal interests.

John 4:1-14   7. Start where the man is, not where you want him to be. We sometimes forget that our language is quite foreign to the sinner in the far country. Such terms as "saved" and "lost" and "born again" need to be explained. Learn the art of asking questions till you have your prospective patient's problem carefully diagnosed. Then prescribe the cure, using not just any scripture but the appropriate scripture for his particular need.

Luke 5:1-11   8. Seek for common interests. To win a landscape gardener, a soul-winner may have to go to the library and read a few books on landscape gardening. Be interested in what men are doing if you expect to get them interested in what you are doing. But always keep alert for the voice of the Spirit in following confidence gained with positive testimony of what Christ means to you. Don't "dilly-dally" too long. Look for opportunities, not excuses, to catch your man for Christ.

Examination on Lesson II

Marks	
6	1. What six conditions for success in soul-winning are set forth in this lesson?
4	2. Suggest at least four additional conditions for success.
20	3. Quote Ps. 51:10-13.
5	4. Quote II Tim. 2:21.
10	5. Use Scripture to show that there is a vital relationship between the indwelling of the Holy Spirit and the living of a clean and separated Christian life.
5	6. How are holiness and happiness related according to your observations from I John 1?
10+3	7. Quote Rom. 12:1, 2. What three conditions for ascertaining the will of God do you find in these two verses?
5+1	8. Quote II Cor. 5:14. What condition for success in soul-winning do you observe from this passage?
5	9. Explain why failure to love God supremely is such a grievous sin in the light of Matt. 22:37, 38.
10+2	10. Quote II Tim. 2:3, 4. Point out how this passage is related to the life of consecration to soul-winning.
5	11. What else beside the love of Christ motivated Paul in his ministry to lost souls according to II Cor. 5:10, 11?
5	12. Illustrate from Scripture or from personal experience how neglect in seeking to win souls to the Saviour may have tragic results.
10	13. Consider carefully how the disciples were prepared for Pentecost. In this connection study chapter one of Acts and explain how it provides a perfect setting for chapter two.
5+5	14. Quote Acts 20:24. From the verse and the context, give a brief account of the compassion of Paul for the lost.
5+3	15. Quote Ps. 126:6. What conditions for success in soul-winning do you observe from this passage?
3	16. Locate the passage that speaks of speaking the truth in love.
5	17. How does a person obtain a passion for lost souls?
5+2	18. Quote Rom. 10:1. What does the verse teach about Paul's prayer ministry in relation to the lost?

Marks

5+2   19. Quote Gal. 4:19. What does the verse teach about Paul's prayer ministry in relation to unstable converts?

6×2   20. Write down your observations of the part played by prayer in revival from the first six chapters of Acts.

11   21. Illustrate from the first chapter of I Samuel how Hannah is a type of a Christian who realizes that barrenness is unnatural and that God has an answer for this problem.

5+5   22. How is importunity in prayer related to soul-winning according to Luke 11 and Luke 18?

15+3   23. Quote Ezek. 3:17, 19. Point out what a solemn responsibility rests upon God's watchmen in the matter of soul-winning.

2+6   24. What is the supreme condition for success in soul-winning? Prove it from Scripture. (Locate two passages.)

5×3   25. Locate Scripture passages to prove the irresistible power of the Holy Spirit in evangelism.

5   26. Quote Eph. 6:17.

5   27. From the account in Acts 8:26-38 show how the personal worker must know the Word in pointing souls to Christ.

15+5   28. Quote II Tim. 2:24-26. Show how the servant of God is to deal with one who tends to be argumentative.

$$\frac{250 \times 100 = 100}{250}$$

LESSON III

SCRIPTURE MEMORIZING FOR SOUL-WINNING

While salvation is a gift, a knowledge of the Scriptures comes by work. The Psalmist testified, "Thy Word have I hid in mine heart that I might not sin against Thee." That was putting a good thing in a good place for a good purpose. But not only is it a distinct advantage to memorize the Word of God for our own spiritual growth but it is indispensable for effective evangelism.

Some students may have been irked by having had to memorize so much scripture in the previous lessons. But the standard need not be lowered. A verse is not really learned until it is known so well that you cannot forget it. Since a good teacher will insist on the accurate quoting of at least every scripture assigned in these lessons, some convenient plan will have to be devised to enable the student to memorize and review till a passage, together with its location, is completely mastered.

Here is a plan that has been tried and proved.

1. Put the passage to be memorized on a card 3" x 1½". Your first card in this course is Matt. 5:14, which will be typed on one side of the card as follows:

> Ye are the light of the world. A city that is set on an hill cannot be hid.

2. On the opposite side of the card put the reference and the number of the card. If you wish, you might include the lesson in which the verse was given.

> L.- 1
>
> 1
>
> Matt. 5:14

Ps. 119:11

25

3. Memorize the verse accurately and know the reference.

4. Put the verses you have just memorized in the front of a cardboard box in a section designated for daily review.

5. When you feel that you have mastered a passage quite well then you may put it in a section behind, designated for weekly review.

6. When you are sure that you know a passage, put it further back in a section designated for monthly review.

7. When you know a verse so well that you cannot forget it, you have it memorized. Such verses may be removed from the box and placed in the archives as a memorial to your accomplishment.

Never give up. Believe in the perseverance of the saints and put your faith into practice in this respect. Your first attempts will be the most difficult but your mind, like your muscle, will grow stronger through exercise. Love the Bible: learn the Bible: then live the Bible.

There are several reasons why Scripture Memorizing is important:

I. *Spiritual progress.*

I Pet. 2:2

II Pet. 3:18

Jer. 15:16

Spiritual progress will be commensurate with the keenness of one's appetite for the Word of God. As an infant cries for milk that he will soon assimilate to sustain and strengthen his body, so the child of God, enjoying spiritual health, will have an insatiable hunger for the Word of God. Loss of appetite for the Word of God is a sure symptom of poor spiritual health.

Heb. 5:11-14

II. *Spirit-endued preaching.*

Heb. 4:12

A sermon, saturated with the Word of God, is persuasive and powerful. When our minds are stored with the Word of God, the Holy Spirit can draw upon these

I Pet. 1:23

Eph. 5:26

II Tim. 4:2

Acts 2

Acts 7

John 14:26

resources to convict and convert. Through the Word of God, men are born again: through the Word, s o u l s are sanctified: through the Word saints are strengthened. Therefore Paul exhorted Timothy to preach the Word. When the Word of God is preached by a servant of God who is filled with the Spirit of God, there will be a revival or a riot. Peter preached and got souls: Stephen preached and got stones. Both preached the Word. And it is obvious that each was able to use the Word from memory. The Spirit will bring to our remembrance truth that has been memorized.

III. *Soul-prosperity.*

Josh. 1:8

Psalm 1

John 14:15

John 14:21

The prosperous soul will take time to memorize and meditate in the Word. God measures success, not in terms of dollars and cents, but in proportion to one's knowledge of and obedience to the Word of God. The memorization of the Word makes possible meditation in the Word by day or by night. But obedience is the transmission that joins truth to conduct. The Word is to be obeyed. That is what makes for soul prosperity. The hymn "Trust and Obey" puts the issue clearly before us:

> Trust and *obey*, for there's no other way
> To be happy in Jesus but to trust and *obey.*

Acts 4:33

John 1:14

Eph. 4:15

I Cor. 13:1

Psalm 1

The memorization of scripture is a minor matter when compared to the importance of living and walking in the spirit of the scriptures. The would-be soul-winner can be a veritable soul-antagonizer if he refuses to let his life be graced and governed by the Spirit of Jesus. Jesus was full of *grace* and truth. Both are needed. But if there is to be a preference, it must be grace first, then truth. If we are unable to speak the truth in love, it might be best to keep silence. Let every soul-winner memorize I Cor. 13, meditate on its truth until the whole spirit is imbued and drenched in the love of Jesus and then let him go forth to witness. Such a person will bring forth fruit in season and whatsoever he doeth will meet with spiritual success.

IV. *Personal testimony.*

Ps. 119:42

When giving personal testimony, it is best to saturate our words with the Word of God. Our words are weak:

Heb. 4:12

Ps. 19:7-8

God's Word is living and powerful. Our words may be inaccurate: but "the testimony of the Lord is sure, mak-

Matt. 7:28-29

ing wise the simple and the statutes of the Lord are right, rejoicing the heart." The best testimony in open-air evan-

Isa. 1:18

gelism and street-meetings is one that rings with the as-

I Thess. 1:5

I Thess. 2:13

surance of divine dictum. The witness must speak with authority. His best authority is *not* his experience: it is the Word. Some testimonies are just vain prattle. They

II Tim. 1:7

lack Holy Ghost conviction. And sometimes the listeners are made to wonder if believers are really believers. If the witness does not believe his beliefs, you can be sure

Acts 5:29

that nobody else will. To be able to look men in the face with a "Thus saith the Lord" will stir and startle sinners

Acts 16:16-18

and lead to their salvation: but an insincere recital of some one else's experience that comes merely from your lips is

Matt. 3:5

more liable to hurry wayward feet to hell. Truth on fire will attract: truth on ice would be better kept in cold

Phil. 2:14-16

storage. When a blameless life holds forth the Word of life, sinners dead in trespasses and sins will be quickened.

Acts 2

Ignite the Word memorized with the fire of the Holy Spirit and soon you will start a mighty conflagration. You may have to get your first pulpit in some wilderness

Matt. 3:3

or on some street corner but if you will pour out God will pour in an abundant supply.

Examination on Lesson III

Marks

5	1. Quote Ps. 119:11.
7	2. What are the seven steps given in this lesson for memorizing a verse of Scripture?
4	3. What four reasons for Scripture Memorizing are given in this lesson?
8	4. Quote and locate a Scripture which shows how a new-born babe in Christ is to grow.
8	5. Quote and locate the verse which shows what the Word of God meant to the prophet Jeremiah.
5	6. Describe in your own words the spiritual condition of those mentioned in Heb. 5:11-14.

7. Locate passages which prove:

3	a. The Word of God is powerful.
3	b. The Word of God is everlasting.
3	c. Men are sanctified by the Word.
3	8. How is one to have success in Christian growth according to Josh. 1:8?
6	9. Contrast the godly with the ungodly from Psalm 1 and show why God is able to bless the godly.
3	10. Where in the Bible does it speak of Jesus being full of grace and truth?
5	11. Quote I Cor. 13:1.
16	12. Quote and locate two passages which speak of the value of using the Word in personal testimony.
8	13. Where in the Bible does it speak of Jesus speaking with authority? Quote the passage.
12	14. How did the Thessalonian church receive Paul's testimony according to I Thess. 1:5 and I Thess. 2:13? Quote each passage and underline the answer.
7	15. Quote II Tim. 1:7. If the spirit of slavish fear does not come from God, where does it come from?
4	16. From your perusal of Matt. 3, write down what you consider to have been the key to such success in the ministry of John the Baptist.
15	17. Quote Phil. 2:14-16.

$$\frac{125 \times 100}{125} = 100$$

LESSON IV

ASSURANCE OF SALVATION

I Thess. 1:5

Rom. 1:14-16

I Cor. 15:1-4

I Cor. 1:18

Tit. 2:11-13

II Cor. 13:5

Heb. 10:38

I John 3:9

Jas. 2:14-17

I Cor. 15:2

I John 2:4

II Tim. 1:9

I Thess. 1:5-6

The gospel came to the church at Thessalonica with "much assurance." The dauntless apostle Paul declared that he was not ashamed to preach such a gospel to anyone, anywhere, because the almighty power of God had been made operative through the gospel in saving every one who believed the good news concerning Christ's substitutionary death, His burial and His resurrection. While the preaching of the cross is to them who perish foolishness, nevertheless, to us who are saved, it is the power of God. Therefore the Christian, claiming to believe that gospel, should be fully assured before God that he has been saved from the penalty of sin; that he is being saved from the power of sin daily; and that he will ultimately be saved from the presence of sin.

Assurance of salvation is not a sedative for the carnal and neither is it a salve for the backslider. The professing Christian who persists in the practice of sin, might better be assured that he is *not* saved. If what one believes does not affect the way one behaves, his faith is vain. The successful soul-winner must know experientially the saving power of Jesus Christ. Not only must *he* be delivered from doubt, but *others* whom he would seek to win, must be convinced of the reality of his being a new creation in Christ Jesus.

In this lesson consideration shall be given to a fourfold ground of assurance. As the four legs of a table are needed for balance, so are these factors essential to a balanced belief in securing a sound scriptural assurance of salvation.

I. *The Word of God.* I John 5:13.

God's Word declares that the believer—

John 3:36
John 3:16

1. Has everlasting life.

31

Acts 13:39
Rom. 5:1   2. Is justified.
Acts 10:43
Acts 13:38   3. Has remission of sins.
John 5:24
John 3:18   4. Shall not come into condemnation.
John 3:16   5. Shall not perish.

John 1:12   6. Has power or authority to speak of himself as a
                    child of God.
Eph. 2:8
John 3:17   7. Is saved.

                    Among other reasons, the apostle John wrote his epis-
I John 5:13   tle that believers might *know* that they have eternal life.
I John 5:10-12   The believer accepts the testimony of God's Word as final
                    and sufficient authority. God cannot lie. His Word is
                    truth. It is not feeling: it is faith. And faith is an as-
Titus 1:2   surance that certain things are exactly as God says they
John 17:17   are. Faith is not hope. It is not hoping for substance.
Heb. 11:1   Faith gives substantial reality to the divine dicta. It is
                    not mere mental assent: it is a moral matter as well. It
                    reaches beyond the head to the heart to the point where
Rom. 10:9-10   head and heart agree that God has spoken the truth.

                    II. *The work of Christ.* Heb. 9:24-10:22.

                    Assurance of salvation is possible on the ground that
                    Jesus Christ has fully satisfied all the holy and righteous
                    demands of God against our sin. In raising Christ from
                    the dead, God has given assurance unto all men that full
Acts 17:31   atonement has been made. God has been reconciled to
                    men: men are urged to be reconciled to God. Any one
                    who discounts the infinite worth of the blood of the spot-
                    less Son of God, cannot have assurance of salvation be-
                    cause:

I John 1:7   1. The blood cleanses us from all sin.

Heb. 9:22   2. Through the blood we have remission for sin.

I Pet. 1:18-19   3. We are redeemed, that is, set free from the bondage
                    and slavery of sin by the blood. Peter also says we are
                    redeemed from vain conversation, that is, aimless living,
                    by the blood, and from traditionalism. That is an im-
                    mense emancipation, to be sure.

Rom. 5:9   4. We are justified by His blood.

Rom. 3:25   5. Through His blood, we have a propitiation for our sin.

In speaking of Christ being a propitiation for our sin, it is meant that in the death of Christ, God's righteous wrath against our sin has been appeased, His justice has been fully satisfied, thus making it possible for God to freely and fully pardon every transgressor, take away all his guilt and give him a righteous standing before a holy God. To refuse Christ as the propitiation for sin is to leave one's soul exposed to the wrath of God: to receive Christ is to be delivered from the wrath to come.

Heb. 10:26 In chapters nine and ten of Hebrews the value of the "one offering" of Christ for sin is seen in contrast to the many offerings made for sin in the Old Testament. In those offerings there was repetition, but not remission; remembrance, but not removal of sin. Through the one sacrifice of Christ sin has been "put away." God's promise

Heb. 10:17 to believers is "Their sins and iniquities will I remember no more."

III. *The witness of the Spirit.* Rom. 8:16 R.V.

There are saints who know they are saved even though they cannot quote and locate a scripture to prove it. There are Christians who know that they are Christians although they could not tell you when or where they were saved. Nevertheless they are as sure of their salvation as they are of their existence. How is that possible? The Holy Spirit assures them that they are God's chil-
John 16:13 dren. The Holy Spirit is the Spirit of truth. He does not lie. His witness is reliable. But there is another spirit, the human spirit, which bears witness along with the Holy Spirit, assuring the believer who is walking in the Spirit, that he is a child of God.

This assurance of sonship and heirship, conveyed to us by the joint-witness of the Holy Spirit and our human spirit, is best attested in the life which experientially knows:

Rom. 8:2   1. Freedom from sin.

Rom. 8:4-5   2. A walk after the Spirit.

Rom. 8:6-7   3. What it means to be spiritually-minded and not carnally-minded.

Rom. 8:14   4. The leading of the Spirit.

Rom. 8:16-18   5. A willingness to suffer now in view of the certainty of glory hereafter.

Rom. 8:26-27   6. An effectual prayer ministry.

Rom. 8:1   This chapter, beginning with no condemnation, end-
Rom. 8:35   ing in no separation and in between having all things
Rom. 8:28   working together for good, represents the normal Chris-
John 15:26-27 tian life as a life lived in constant dependence on the
Acts 5:32   Holy Spirit. When such a person bears witness of the sav-
              ing power of Christ, the Spirit joins in and gives His
John 16:7-11   testimony too, worldlings are convicted, convinced and
Acts 6:10   converted and Christ is glorified. Such witness is irresis-
              tible. Such assurance can be the portion and privilege
Gal. 4:4-6   of every redeemed sinner.

              IV. *The wonder of a transformed life.* II Cor. 5:17.

              It took a miracle to create the world. It takes a miracle
Genesis 1   to transform a sinner into a saint. And each time a sinner
II Cor. 5:17 is converted to Jesus Christ, God works a miracle of
              transformation. Among other evidences of a genuine con-
              version, there should be the following:

II Cor. 6:14-18   1. A desire for fellowship with God's children.

I John 3:14
I John 5:1   2. A genuine love for all members of His family.

I John 2:4   3. A life of obedience.

I John 2:15   4. A love for God that displaces love for the world
              and the things of the world.

I John 2:29   5. Right living.

                  6. A cessation of the practice of sin.
I John 3:9
              It is to be feared that many professors of salvation
              are not possessors. If the Bible standard is accepted as

the criterion for distinguishing things that differ, then Christendom abounds with pretenders and hypocrites. John, the apostle of love, declared with apostolic authority that men were liars if their life did not tally with their lip. Though not judges, we are fruit inspectors. Wheat and tares may be allowed to grow together till harvest, but there will be an accurate segregation in that day.

Matt. 7:15-20
Matt. 13:30
Rom. 2:16

Some people may get converted to a church, a creed, a denomination, an evangelist or to a preacher, but unless one is converted to Jesus Christ, it will avail nothing. One of the greatest hindrances in soul-winning effort, is the inconsistent living on the part of those professing to know Him. On the other hand, there is no argument more convincing to an unsaved soul than the experience of meeting a truly transformed life, made radiant and beautiful by the mighty miracle of salvation. The best apologetic for the gospel is a transformed life.

I Thess. 1:9
Matt. 18:3

Matt. 5:14

Examination on Lesson IV

Marks	
4	1. What four-fold ground of assurance is set forth in this lesson?
15+3	2. Quote Rom. 1:14-16. Why was not Paul ashamed to preach the gospel in imperial Rome?
3	3. What is the gospel according to I Cor. 15:1-4?
5	4. Quote I Cor. 1:18.
7×1	5. According to Tit. 2:11-13, what does the grace of God do with respect to our past, present and future?
2×3	6. What is the purpose of the exhortation given in II Cor. 13:5 and Heb. 10:38?
4	7. Explain what you think the Bible means when it speaks of believing in vain.
5	8. Quote I John 5:13.

9. Quote each of the following verses and in each case tell what assurance is given to the believer:

10×5	a. John 3:36.
10×1	b. John 3:16.
	c. Acts 13:39.
	d. Rom. 5:1.
	e. Acts 10:43.
	f. John 5:24.
	g. John 3:18.
	h. John 1:12.
	i. Eph. 2:8.
	j. I John 5:13.

10. How is the shed blood of Christ related to the subject of assurance according to:

6×5	a. I John 1:7.
6×1	b. Heb. 9:22.
	c. I Pet. 1:18-19.
	d. Rom. 5:9.
	e. Rom. 3:25.

5	11. What is the meaning and significance of propitiation?
6	12. How does the finished work of Christ on the cross compare with the unfinished works of O. T. priests?
5+2	13. Quote Rom. 8:16. What two-fold assurance of sonship is mentioned in this passage?

Marks

6×2   14. Mention at least six ways in which the Holy Spirit assures a believer in Christ that he belongs to God's family.

5+2   15. Quote Acts 5:32. How is this verse related to the subject of our witnessing?

2   16. On whom must the Christian depend in convicting the world of sin, righteousness and judgment?

5   17. Quote II Cor. 5:17.

       18. Quote the following passages and in each case tell how the verse proves that a miracle of transformation has been wrought in the life.

5×5   a. I John 3:14.
5×2   b. I John 2:4.
              c. I John 5:1.
              d. I John 2:29.
              e. I John 3:9.

3   19. Where is the passage that assures us that we can know whether a man is good or corrupt just as surely as we can discern a grapevine from a thorn bush?

3   20. What does I Thess. 1:9 teach about conversion?

5   21. Quote Matt. 18:3.

$238 \times \dfrac{100}{238} = 100$

LESSON V

THE LIFE OF VICTORY

I Cor. 3:1

What It Is

Paul, in his letter to the Corinthian church, draws a distinction between two classes of Christians, the carnal and the spiritual. A carnal Christian is a spiritual infant. As such, his life is self-centered, not Christ-centered. His discomforts and displeasures are loudly advertised anytime and anywhere. He may at times be a sweet little darling if cuddled, cooed and comforted at the least sign of his dislike but he never seems to grow up. The carnal Christian, like old king Saul, is full of jealousy. Therefore he carries a javelin in his hand to use with deadly effect on every one he imagines might topple him from his throne.

I Cor. 3:3
I Cor. 3:4
I Cor. 5:2
Heb. 5:12

Heb. 10:32-36

Heb. 5:14

The carnal Christian, being a divider, sows discord among the brethren. He is factious, sectarian and proud. He may have had a very vital experience in the hazy past but it has been allowed to grow anaemic and lifeless in the present. Having advanced to the place where he was taking solid food at one time, he has suffered a spiritual relapse and has to be put back on a milk diet. He is sluggish in his responses to divine directions. All of this is strictly out of accord with the spiritual standard set forth in the New Testament. Therefore it is imperative that every one, calling himself Christian, should depart from iniquity. A child of God is expected to bear the image of his Father.

II Tim. 2:19

Rom. 8:29

Rom. 6:14

II Cor. 2:14

The normal New Testament ideal for every child of God is a life of victory over sin, self and Satan. Such a life is not to be casual but continual. It is presented under various types and figures throughout the Scriptures. The name of the experience that brings a person into the conscious realization of Christ enthroned within the heart, is not nearly as important as the knowledge that

it *is* so. As conflict precedes conquest and as battle is the
prelude to victory, so it is in Christian experience. The
self-life, in its struggle against the Spirit, will elicit a
strong cry, "Who shall deliver me?" before the clear answer comes, "Thank God through Jesus Christ our Lord."

Rom. 7:24-25

I. *Old Testament portraits.* There are many pictures of
the victorious life in the Old Testament:

1. It is walking with God. Gen. 5:22; Heb. 11:5.
Enoch did not walk with God till after he begat Methu-
selah. The experience lasted for 300 years.

2. It is casting out the bondwoman and her son. Gen.
16; Gen. 21; Gal 4:30-31. The ceaseless conflict between Ishmael and Isaac, Hagar and Sarah, is typical of
the conflict in many hearts between the flesh and the
spirit. Thank God, there can be a day of deliverance!

Gal. 5:17
Rom. 7:24-25

3. It is crossing the Jordan. Josh. 1:2; Heb. 4:1. Some
Christians wander aimlessly for years in a waste howling
wilderness. God's purpose was to bring His people *out of*
Egyptian bondage and *into* Canaan (Deut. 8:7-10). The
conquest of Canaan could not be realized till Jordan was
crossed.

Heb. 3-4
Josh. 1:1-2

4. It is Gilgal. Josh. 5; Col. 2:11. Gilgal was the
place of circumcision. Circumcision, the putting away of
the sins of the flesh, speaks of the utter helplessness of
God's people to achieve victory and thus our complete dependence on the Lord for the conquest of the land.

Josh. 5:2-9
Col. 2:11

5. As God requires the putting off of the old man
and the putting on of the new man, as the crucifixion
of the flesh must precede the resurrection to new life,
so all down through Old Testament history it is revealed
that it is (a) not Adam but Christ, (b) not Cain but
Abel, (c) not Ishmael but Isaac, (d) not Esau but Jacob,
(e) not Manasseh but Ephraim, (f) not Moses but Josh-
ua, (g) not Saul but David, (h) not Adonijah but Solo-
mon. This all serves to teach the basic principle of victorious Christian living, "Not I, but Christ."

Eph. 4:22-24

Rom. 5:12-21

Gal. 2:20

II. *New Testament portrayals.* There are many different descriptions of the victorious life in the New Testament. To mention a few, it is:

1. The yielded life. Rom. 6:13; Rom. 12:1-2.

The use of the aorist tense in the Greek word, *parastesate,* translated "yield" with reference to God, directs attention to the action as pointed or punctiliar. The action in verse 16 however is continuous, being a present durative, *paristanete.* Generally speaking at least, there is a point in the normal Christian life where he ceases to struggle in his own strength to control his members and hands over the government of his passions to the only ONE Who can master them, the Lord Jesus Christ. But the initial committal is to be followed by daily committals. A life once truly yielded will have no difficulty in continuing to yield.

Luke 9:23

2. It is the sanctified life. II Cor. 7:1; I Thess. 4:3, 7.

The victorious life provides victory over the world. By the world is meant human life and society with God ruled out, or, that Satanic system which insidiously labors to alienate our souls from God by providing all manner of allurements and attractions which stifle spiritual growth. In II Cor. 6:14-18, Christians are commanded to "Come out from among them" and the promise is given to the obedient, "I will receive you *and* will be a Father unto you *and* ye shall be my sons and daughters, saith the Lord Almighty."

I John 5:4

Eph. 2:1-3

Then it goes right on in chapter 7 to admonish God's people to *cleanse* themselves from all filthiness of the flesh *and spirit.* Again, the Greek verb is an aorist tense and emphasizes the need for a crucial transaction, a definite dealing, an act that will not require repetition. But it is followed by another present durative verb which indicates the need for constant vigilance in the pursuit of holiness and purity of life. This gives the proper balance. An experience ten years ago that is not producing good fruit today is worthless. The author is more interested in seeing victorious *lives* than he is of hearing

II Cor. 7:1

of victorious experiences that are contradicted by present behaviour.

3. It is a dedicated life. Rom. 12:1-2.

The presentation of our body to God, the Holy Spirit is to be a definite committal; but again, the act is to be followed by an attitude. It is to be presented as a *living* sacrifice. When once the life has been dedicated to God, no one must presume to take from the altar of *God,* what has been presented to *God.* It is His forever, only *His.* It is daring daylight robbery to take from God what is now His. Such an act should not be done lightly. But it should be our daily worship to live in the realization of His manifold mercies and His infinite grace and in the attitude that we are *His* alone.

4. It is a Spirit-filled life. Eph. 5:18; Acts 2:4.

Pentecost must be more than just an historical event. The disciples were filled with the Holy Spirit on the day of Pentecost and from that day their lives were truly transformed. Calvary is an historical event too but its meaning is realized only by those who have experiential knowledge of salvation. The filling with the Holy Spirit was crucial but there were other crucial fillings. The use of the Greek aorist tense in 4:8, 31; 9:17; 10:44; 11:15; 13:9 indicate that the experience was climactic and crucial. But the state of one who has been filled is that he will be "full of the Holy Ghost." This experience of the constant fulness of the Spirit is referred to in the following passages: Acts 6:3-5; 11:24; 13:52; Eph. 5:18; John 7:37-39.

5. It is the crucified life. Rom. 6:10-11; Gal. 2:20.

There is something very crucial about death. It represents the end of a certain kind of life. In this lesson, it speaks of the end of the self-life, which is the very quintessence of a sinful life. Selfishness is sin. The lair of all evil lies in the self-life. The only cure for this malady is death. But while the death of the old man is crucial, there is to be a daily reckoning of the reality of Christ's crucifixion of the flesh at Calvary.

Rom. 6:2, 11
6. It is the resurrected life. Rom. 6:4, 11; Col. 3:1.

Luke 24:17

Luke 24:25

Luke 24:31-32
The victorious Christian is dead to sin, but alive to God. The living Lord, triumphant over all the power of the enemy, is risen indeed. There are many discouraged disciples walking the Emmaus road today. Their unbelief and hardness of heart have blinded their eyes. They need a heart-warming and an eye-opening that only Christ Himself can impart. Although the truth of the resurrection had been imbedded in the Old Testament Scriptures for centuries and Christ Himself had spoken plainly of His resurrection during His ministry to the disciples, yet to them, the truth had never been realized. But there was a day, an hour, a moment when the risen Redeemer was revealed. Convinced of that fact, the disciples went forth to witness to a hostile world and millions were converted. That conviction will still move disciples of Christ to witness. Meeting the risen Lord was a crucial experience that resulted in a fruitful ministry of soul-winning.

The story is told that Mrs. Martin Luther, on seeing her husband very discouraged one day, put a black crepe on the doorknob. When the great reformer enquired who had died, she replied, "I thought perhaps that God had died since you were so disconsolate." There are too many such Christians. Their unbelief renders them miserable. To know the power of His resurrection in the life, is victory.

7. It is the reigning life. Rom. 5:17; 6:14; Rev. 12:11.

Gen. 1:26, 28

Rom. 5:21

Rom. 5:17
God's original purpose for man was that he should have dominion. When sin entered, that dominion was forfeited. Christ, the last Adam, has regained in redemption what man lost in the Fall. His grace is that inward provision that meets every outward circumstance. When a Christian is willing to abdicate and yield his right to reign to the King of kings, even Christ, at that point the government of the life is transferred from self to the Saviour. In Christ, the Christian can be *more* than conqueror. Through Christ, sin need not have dominion.

Rom. 8:35-39
Rom. 6:14
Rev. 12:11
Acts 6:15
Acts 7:59
Phil. 1:13

Acts 20:24
By the blood of Christ and by the word of his testimony, the child of God can be an overcomer even *in* death, as well as *unto* death. Even though a prisoner, the apostle Paul was a prince. He wrote the great epistle of joy to the Philippian church when he was a prisoner at Rome. He was able to finish his course with joy because Christ reigned in such full measure that he regarded himself as *His* prisoner.

8. It is a life of rest. Heb. 4:10; Matt. 11:29-30.

Josh. 1:15

Heb. 11:30

Heb. 4:10
There are two rests referred to in Matt. 11:28-30. The first rest has to do with salvation: the second with service. Canaan was to be to Israel a place of rest. Certainly it was not a place of physical rest. But it was a place where Israel was to see the wonder-working power of God exercised on their behalf. Their duty was to trust and obey: God's working was according to their faith. When man ceases his working, that is, his self-efforts, the Lord begins to work. Truly, no man can work like He can!

Examination on Lesson V

Marks	
2	1. What two classes of Christians does Paul mention?
5	2. Describe one of these classes.
4+20	3. What are a few of the Old Testament portraits of the victorious life? Explain the significance of four of these pictures of victorious Christian living.
10	4. Explain from Rom. 6:13, 16 what the yielded life is.
10	5. Explain II Cor. 7:1 in the light of its context and make clear its application to victorious living.
35	6. Quote II Cor. 6:14-18 and I Thess. 4:3, 7.
10+5	7. Quote Rom. 12:1, 2 and make clear how you would use this passage to show what is meant by the life of victory.
15	8. Make clear the difference between the experience of being filled with the Holy Spirit and the state resulting from the experience.
20	9. Quote Eph. 5:18 and John 7:37-39.
10	10. Explain what you mean by a crucified life. Illustrate what you mean by Scripture, personal experience or any other source.
5	11. Quote Rom. 6:11.
10	12. How is the resurrection of Christ related to victorious Christian living?
5	13. What was God's original purpose for man according to Gen. 1:26, 28?
5	14. What hindered the immediate realization of that purpose?
5	15. How does grace intervene to make victory over sin possible?
5	16. In what circumstances was Paul more than conqueror according to Rom. 8:35-39?
15+4	17. Quote Matt. 11:29-30 and Heb. 4:10 and make clear what is meant by the life of rest.

$$200 \times \frac{100}{200} = 100$$

LESSON VI

THE LIFE OF VICTORY (Continued)

How To Enter In

Defeat in living the Christian life will stop and stifle effective soul-winning. Therefore no apology is made for taking two lessons on this theme. Even though there were many indirect suggestions in the previous lesson on the nature of victorious Christian living, the subject has so many aspects that one feels warranted in giving separate treatment to the practical side of the subject by showing the hungry-hearted how they may enter in. Those who consider that they are "rich and increased with goods and have need of nothing" will find little help here. God can bless the poor in spirit, but the rich He will send empty away. Laodicean lukewarmness is nauseating to God. The most needy people in our churches are those who are least conscious of any need.

Rev. 3:17
Luke 1:53

Rev. 3:16

It is wrong to be involved in controversy over terminology, especially in respect to victorious Christian living. A blameless life is worth more than a library full of arguments. Some people contend for the truth but manifest little grace when opposed. Jesus was "full of grace and truth." The best evidence of being filled with the Spirit, is to be imbued with the spirit of Jesus. Jesus came to give His life to save men. One who is filled with His Spirit will live to seek and to save that which is lost.

John 1:14
Matt. 20:28

Luke 19:10

In this lesson, there are four windows in the door leading into the great living-room of the deeper life, *admit, submit, commit* and *transmit*. Each will help us to see a little more of the meaning and message of the abundant life. A correspondent student, after studying this lesson and while preparing to write the examination on it, got down on her knees before the Lord, claimed the promise of the Spirit's fulness, and then wrote the test. Her glowing report of how God had so definitely met her need,

47

was abundant compensation for the time taken to write the lesson. May many more cross their Jordans and enter Canaan.

The steps leading into the sanctuary of a holy life may be many or few. No mechanical method can be devised to direct a Christian out of the mire of defeat to the firm foundation of victorious Christian living. Each of the four principles set forth in this lesson, is intended to be as a window, admitting light to the life as it shines forth from the lamp of God's Word.

I. *Admit:*

1. Your need. Isa. 41:17; 44:3; Matt. 5:6; John 7:37.

The admission of need must be very genuine. The Spirit of God, speaking in the prophet Isaiah, likens the preparation of the soul to a man perishing with thirst. God does not waste His blessings. God is not extravagant. God will supply all our *need*. A man dying of thirst, *must* have water. A land under the seizure of dust and drought, so dry that even the beasts of the field cry to God for water, is in desperate need of rain. When the prophet Joel saw the need of Zion, he called for national mourning and genuine repentance before making any promise of rain and relief. The church must do the same. The individual Christian must truly repent before he can experience revival in his own soul. Christ did not say "Blessed are they who have wealth" or "Blessed are they who have health" or "Blessed are they who know the doctrines of the deeper life," but rather "Blessed are they which do hunger and thirst after righteousness, for they shall be filled." The history of revivals demonstrates that God does not pour out His Spirit in profusion upon any church or any community until some see that the need is so desperate that divine help is imperative.

Phil. 4:19
Matt. 5:6
Joel 1:20

Joel 2:12-19
II Chron. 7:14
Rev. 2-3

Matt. 5

James 5:16-18

2. God's provision. Luke 11:1-13; John 7:37-39.

The promise of the Spirit in Luke 11:13, is found in a context which reveals the importance of importunate

Luke 24:49

Luke 3:21

Acts 1:14

Acts 4:31

Gal. 3:2, 5

praying before the blessing is bestowed. A prayerless person is never prepared for any genuine experience with the Holy Ghost. Jesus was praying when the heaven was opened and the Holy Ghost descended. The disciples had been praying before the Spirit came upon them at Pentecost. The church was having a prayer meeting when the house was shaken and members were filled with the Spirit. Wherever there is a real recognition of need, there will always be the divine provision. The praying soul will reach a place of rest in his communion with God where he can in simple faith reach out and claim the promise.

II. *Submit:*

1. To God. Rom. 12:1; Rom. 6:13.

Gen. 32:24-28

The reconciling of a soul to God to the point where there is "perfect submission" and "all is at rest" is a tedious task. The tendency of the flesh is to resist God. The flesh, at enmity with God, will fight and fuss and persistently refuse to yield to the sovereign will of God. To enter into victory, one must give up the struggle and yield to God in utter surrender. Jacob saw at last that he could not prevail against the angel that wrestled with him for a whole night. Finally with thigh out of joint, in utter helplessness, he yielded to God and became a different individual. As a typewriter responds to the touch of the typist, so as instruments in His hands, children of God are to be subject to His control.

2. To Christ. Luke 6:46.

Eph. 4:5

The recognition of the Lordship of Christ is the norm for all believers. "There is *one* Lord." The constant confusion in the minds of some saints is traceable to their never having settled the question of the mastery of their lives.

3. To the Holy Spirit. Rom. 8:14.

Some professing Christians are like a wild horse on the range. They have never been "broken." Once broken, they can be led. The victorious Christian has met this issue and yielded control to a divine person, the blessed Holy Spirit.

III. *Commit:*

1. Your past. I John 1:9.

God needs clean vessels to fill with His Holy Spirit. The sins and failures of the past must be faithfully dealt with. Where this involves the restitution of goods taken, the confession of wrong done or whatever is needed to set the house in order, it must be done. But when one has confessed his sins to God, he is to rest assured that God, according to His own promise, has forgiven him and has cleansed him from all unrighteousness.

Num. 5:5-7
Lev. 6:1-7
Matt. 5:23-24

2. Your possessions. Mark 10:29-30.

Family, friends, desire for fame and fortune, the flesh and all its offspring, must never be allowed to alienate the true disciple of Christ from his high and holy calling. Whether it is the farm or the firm, the position or the profession, the call to follow Him is to be prompt. There is no cheap consecration. It costs nothing to be saved but it costs everything to follow Christ after being saved. But the divine dividends are colossal—even a hundredfold, that is, one hundred times as much as you invest. In terms of mathematics, it is interest at ten thousand per cent. In God's arithmetic, to lose all is to gain all and to divide everything is to have your blessings multiplied. No one can lose who is loosed from his attachments here in order to be bound for life to the good and perfect and acceptable will of God.

Matt. 9:9
Eph. 2:8-9
Mark 10:28
Luke 14:33
Mark 10:30

Luke 6:38

Rom. 12:2

IV. *Transmit:*

1. To the church the benefits of your consecration. I Cor. 12:12-27; Matt. 3:11; Gal. 5:22-23; 6:1-2.

Consecration that has a terminus at the front of a church, in a prayer room, or any other sacred place, is vain. God wants saints who will both worship Him and work for Him. It is mere sentiment to say that one loves the Lord and then is unwilling to do what He says. To meet God in an upper room is wonderful but

John 20:19-22

to remain behind closed doors while sinners perish, is criminal. God gives the Holy Spirit to them who obey Him. His clear command to the church is to go into all the world to preach the gospel to every creature.

Gal. 6:1-2

He that is spiritual will be burdened to minister to the sick saints, not only the physically sick but the spiritually sick. There are many wounded spirits who need nursing back to spiritual health. If one can find an outlet for the flowing of the living waters, God will see to it that there will never be any lack of supply. The filling of the Holy Spirit will make Christians a blessing to the church. Let those who are seeking the blessing of the sanctified, Spirit-filled and victorious Christian life, have as their motive, being a blessing to others.

2. To the world. Acts 1:8; Rom. 1:14-16.

Rom. 1:14

Christians are in debt. They owe the gospel to the whole wide world. The evidence that one has been filled with the Spirit is that he *is* a witness by lip and life everywhere he goes.

Examination on Lesson VI

Marks	
15	1. Quote Isa. 41:17 and 44:3 and explain from these passages what are the pre-requisites for entrance upon a victorious Christian life.
10	2. From a brief survey of the book of Joel, the prophet of Pentecost, how are drought and desolation related to repentance and revival?
5	3. Mention a few of the conditions for blessing contained in the Beatitudes of Matt. 5:1-14.
5	4. How did Elijah get rain according to James 5:16-18? Do you see any parallel in this for the church?
5	5. In your own words explain the context of Luke 11:13.
15	6. Quote John 7:37-39.
10	7. How do you intend to apply these passages in helping one to enter the abundant life?
15	8. Quote Rom. 12:1 and 6:13 and make clear what is meant by submission. Why is it so difficult to bring souls to the point of full surrender to the will of God?
5	9. How does recognition of the Lordship of Christ help to settle the confusion in many minds about life decisions?
10	10. Quote Rom. 8:14. What does this verse teach about the Holy Spirit and our relationship to Him? Think it through.
10	11. Quote I John 1:9. How may the past mar the present and darken the future according to the context?
15	12. Quote Mark 10:29-30. What inducement to consecration do you find in this passage?
10	13. Mention some of the blessings a Christian has to transmit to the church according to the passages cited.
20	14. To whom are Christians in debt according to Rom. 1:14-15 and how is one to pay this debt? Quote Rom. 1:14-16.

$$150 \times \frac{100}{150} = 100$$

Summary of Part I

The purpose of the first six lessons of this soul-winning series, is to prepare recruits, spiritually, for front-line action. The next series of studies will provide methods and mental equipment for participation in evangelism. Before commencing the new phase of study, let every student enquire diligently, "Is Christ satisfied with my life at this moment?" Are you clean, consecrated, compassionate, living in constant communion with God? Have you been filled with the Spirit? Are you too busy to memorize Scripture, to ponder His Word and saturate your soul with its exquisite delights? Are you fully assured from His Word, His work, His Spirit and the transformation in your life that you have been truly born again according to New Testament standards? Are you living in victory? Are you carnal or are you spiritual? Have you yielded to God in everything? Have you let the Holy Spirit take over the mastery of all you have and are? Have you received grace for grace? Have you abdicated the throne of your heart and have you crowned Christ Lord of all? Is the conflict past? Does peace reign? If not, at this very moment give God everything for keeps and then be renewed in the spirit of this devotion daily.

PART II
PARTICIPATION IN SOUL-WINNING

LESSON VII

DEALING WITH CHILDREN

I. *The precedence of child evangelism.*

The late Dr. Charles Haddon Spurgeon wrote in the book *Early Conversion:*

> Some hinder the children because they are forgetful of the child's value. The soul's price does not depend upon its years. God forgive those who despise the little ones. Will you be angry with me if I say that a boy is more worth saving than a man? It is infinite mercy on God's part to save those who are seventy; for what good can they now do with the fag-end of their lives? When we get to be fifty or sixty we are almost worn out and if we have spent all our early days with the devil, what remains for God? But these dear boys and girls . . . there is something to be made out of them. If now they yield themselves to Christ they may have a long, happy and holy day before them in which they may serve God with all their hearts.

I Tim. 3:4-5

II Tim. 1:5

II Tim. 3:15

It is the conviction of the writer of this course that every Christian church and every Christian home should have as an objective the definite salvation of every child before it reaches the troublous teens. The Holy Spirit will guide concerning the time and season to pluck this precious fruit. But children ripen very soon in the warm atmosphere of a genuine Christian home,

Matt. 18:6-9

especially when the fire of sanctified zeal is burning brightly in the church as well. It is a very serious matter when adults in the home or the church act in such a way as to cause little ones to stumble. Parents, claiming

Ps. 105:15

to love their children while at the same time proclaiming their malice and hatred for the preacher and other children of God, are guilty of murder. How tragic the thought that a parent could be the murderer of his

I John 3:15

own children and thus occasioning the eternal loss of

their soul. Child evangelism should be a strong incentive to any church and to any home to live blamelessly before God for the children's sake as well as for Christ's sake.

The importance of winning children to Christ is clearly set forth in the teachings of Christ. All three synoptic gospels speak of Christ's tender dealings with mothers and their little children. The word "little" is used repeatedly in Matt. 18:1-14; 19:13-15; Mark 10:13-16; Luke 18:15-17. Our Lord's commands, "Forbid them not" and "Despise them not" and His solemn warning about offending "one of these little ones" demand our reverential attention. Jesus taught that little ones might perish. His parable about the lost sheep in Matt. 18:10-14 makes it very plain that He had reference to the loss of a little child. He talked of "these little ones which *believe* in me" indicating that little ones can be believers. He pleaded that the little ones be suffered to come unto Him showing that they were old enough to at least come and believe. The simplicity of salvation is thereby revealed to adults who must come to Jesus and believe in Him if they are to be saved.

The age of conversion is nowhere given in the Bible. But a poem by Edith Goreham Clark, published in *Sunday School Times* puts the matter before us very tenderly and beautifully:

Matt. 19:14

Matt. 18:10

Matt. 18:6

How Old Ought I to Be?

"Dear Mother," said a little maid,
"Please whisper it to me,
Before I am a Christian
How old ought I to be?"

"How old ought you to be, dear child,
Before you can love me?"
"I always loved you, Mother mine,
Since I was tiny wee.

"I love you now and always will,"
The little daughter said,
And on her Mother's shoulder laid
Her golden, curly head.

"How old, my girlie, must you be,
Before you trust my care?"
"O Mother dear, I do, I do,
I trust you everywhere."

"How old ought you to be, my child,
To do the things I say?"
The little girl looked up and said,
"I can do that today."

"Then you can be a Christian, too,
Don't wait till you are grown:
Tell Jesus now you come to Him,
To be His very own."

Then as the little maid knelt down
And said, "Lord, if I may,
I'd like to be a Christian now."
He answered, "Yes, today."

II. *A way of procedure in child evangelism.*

When through prayer and instruction in the simple truths of the gospel, it is evident that the Spirit of God is at work in a child's heart, a teacher or parent or any one who has won the confidence of the child in things spiritual, may make a direct approach to the child by asking, "Would you like to receive God's greatest gift, the Lord Jesus Christ into your heart?" If the child is ripe and ready to answer "Yes" then take a Bible, seek for a quiet and secluded place, if possible, and proceed as follows-:

Rev. 3:20

1. Begin the interview with prayer.

2. Place a Bible or Testament in the child's hand and allow him to read aloud the verse found in Rom. 3:23. You may ask, "How many does God say have sinned?" "Does that include you?" "Read the verse as though it were talking just of you, using the word 'I' instead of 'All.' "

3. "Now let us read another verse, Rom. 6:23. 'Wages' means what one earns or deserves. Your father receives wages for the work he does. This verse tells us that those who have sinned, earn or deserve wages and the wages of sin is death. The word 'death' does

not mean physical death in the sense that people die and are buried. The verse places before you a choice between eternal death and eternal life. Eternal death is eternal separation from God: eternal life is eternal fellowship with God. Would you want to be separated from God for ever and ever or would you like to have God with you for ever and ever?"

4. If the child is ready to receive God's gift, the Lord Jesus Christ, you might turn to John 1:12. Allow him to read the verse. Lead to a definite decision.

5. Conclude with John 3:16, using it to show that the one who believes and receives God's gift, has eternal life.

6. Encourage him to read a portion of God's Word each day. For a small sum of money, Scripture Union notes from Inter-Varsity Christian Fellowship, 30 Mary St., Toronto, Canada provide a plan for the systematic reading of the Scriptures and also has notes on the portion read, suited to all age groups.

7. See to it that the child has a Bible, obtain his name and address and get him interested in attending Sunday School, if not attending already.

8. The child, in company and co-operation with the parents, should be encouraged to adopt a church home where he may grow in grace and in the knowledge of his Lord and Saviour also through the ministry of the Word in the church services.

III. *Some general principles for dealing with children.*

1. Deal with children alone if possible.

2. Always use the Word of God.

3. Use only a few verses of Scripture which have similar terms.

4. Always give a portion of the Word for conviction of sin and for assurance of salvation.

5. Lead to a definite decision with an understanding in the child's heart of what has taken place.

6. The child should have assurance of salvation before leaving.

7. The child should be led to pray.

8. The child should confess Christ to his or her friends.

9. The child should be encouraged to win others to the Saviour.

10. A Junior Prayer Band should be established in every evangelical church and opportunity given weekly for prayer, testimony and suitable Christian service. This can become the most enthusiastic group in the church and the children will have as many answers to prayer as the adults.

Examination on Lesson VII

Marks	
5	1. Express in your own words what attitude Spurgeon held with respect to early conversion.
5	2. What advantages did Timothy have with respect to home training? Do you recall any disadvantages?
5	3. Quote II Tim. 3:15.
5	4. Why is adult attitude and behaviour toward children who believe such a serious matter according to Christ?
5	5. Why is it wrong for church members to speak harmfully of their pastor before their children?
10	6. Mention at least five things taught by our Lord concerning Child Evangelism.
5 × 8	7. Make clear what steps you should take in leading a child to Christ.
11	8. Indicate what you intend to do with respect to follow-up work after you have led a child to Christ.
7 × 2	9. Mention at least seven general principles that should be observed in dealing with children.

——
100

LESSON VIII

DEALING WITH THE CONCERNED

John 2:23-25

John 12:42-43

James 2:19

Acts 16:30-31

Acts 1:14
Acts 2:42-47
Acts 4:24-32
Acts 6:4
Acts 13:3

I John 2:4
2:9; 2:15
3:9-10; 3:14;
5:4

Matt. 8:18-22

There is a tendency toward an "easy believism" in some circles when dealing with souls, making it necessary to say a word against such shallow and superficial soul-sinning. Not until the Spirit of God has been allowed to do a thorough work of conviction, not until a soul is convinced that he is hopelessly lost apart from Jesus Christ, is it wise to use such a verse as "Believe on the Lord Jesus Christ and thou shalt be saved."

Our lesson deals with the *concerned*. That concern must be deep. To create that concern will invariably involve soul-travail in prayer. The church will not prevail if she refuses to travail. It is becoming a veritable plague in evangelical circles to hold series after series of evangelistic campaigns before proper prayer preparation. And the results of such series of meetings prove the vanity of such waste of time and expenditure of money.

There is no evangelist on the face of the earth who can effect any lasting result in the salvation of souls apart from much prayer, mighty prayer and more prayer. Souls professing conversion in a prayerless atmosphere, are still-born, not Spirit-born. And every such profession that falls short of sure possession, is tragic enough to make the angels weep, not rejoice. The so-called backsliding, carnality and worldliness corrupting our evangelical churches is attributable too often to a pastor's or evangelist's lust for self-aggrandizement. When the acid test of Scripture is applied to the lives and experience of many members of evangelical churches today, the conclusion must be drawn in the light of the teaching of such scripture found in the first Epistle of John that they were never truly born again.

Did not Jesus discourage hasty discipleship? Did He not demand that people count the cost before assuming

63

Luke 14:25-33
John 6:66-68

Matt. 28:19

John 15:14

Acts 2:37
Acts 16:30

Acts 10

to be one of His followers? And how dare a man profess to be a *follower* of Jesus Christ while standing and sinking in the mire of immorality, dishonesty and debauchery? Jesus commissioned the church to *teach* all nations to *observe all things which He commanded them.* The church has majored on the promises of God and minored on the commandments. Jesus said, "Ye are my friends if ye *do* whatsoever I command you."

When it is clear that the Spirit has done a real preparatory work in convicting a soul of his need of salvation, invoking such concern that the person has expressed a desire to seek God and His salvation, then it is best to limit the discussion to a very few passages of scripture that have one dominant theme.

I. *Short sermons for sincere seekers.*

A. *From the epistle of Paul to the Romans.*

1. Turn in your Bible to chapter 3 and re a d slowly from verse 9 to verse 20. This will enable the counsellor to diagnose the reality of the sense of need in the enquirer and it will lay a firm foundation for the presentation of salvation. Go on to verse 23 and make a personal application.

Soul-winning is *personal* work. Make it personal by having the person read the verse this way, "*I* have sinned and *I* have come short of the glory of God." Sin can only be measured by comparing sinful man to a holy God. It is our *unlikeness* to God as seen in contrast to the "likeness" of original man. The *Fall* of Man has put a vast moral distance between the creature and the Creator. The hymn-writer saw this clearly when he wrote, "O the *mighty* gulf that God did span at Calvary!" Sin is that wicked principle in the human heart that has alienated man from his God, putting an impassable gulf between them. Christ alone can bridge the gap. His death makes possible man's reconciliation and return to fellowship.

2. Now turn to chapter 5 and read verses 6-8. This is *good* news for one who has believed the *bad* news.

Gen. 1:26
Eph. 4:24

Eph. 2:12
Isa. 59:1-2
Eph. 2:13
Eph. 2:14

Rom. 5:6-8

Rom. 3:9, 19

I Tim. 1:15

Salvation is for sinners only, for sinners lost and hopeless, *"without* strength" and without God, "the ungodly." An "ungodly" man is not necessarily limited to the class who curse and cuss and consume champagne. An "ungodly" man is the one who has been deceived into thinking that he can live without God. Such people live in a fool's paradise. To live as though we were not dependent on God for everything, is to act as though we were God. He alone is absolute. Without *Him* man is destitute, lost and hopeless.

Focus attention on the clause, "Christ died for us." Make it personal, "Christ died for *me*." Tarry till it is clear to the enquirer *Who* died, *why* Christ died, and for *whom* Christ died. One might go on to verse 9 and emphasize the "blood" as the only ground of justification, that is, a right relationship to God made possible by the full satisfaction of His righteousness.

3. By turning finally to chapter 6 and verse 23, the enquirer might be led to a definite decision. A giver implies a receiver. It does not take long to receive a gift. "The gift of God is eternal life." No one can pay for a gift but the giver. It costs the receiver nothing. God is the Giver. He gives eternal life. Invite the seeker to receive God's unspeakable gift, eternal life. Christ is that eternal life.

John 3:16

I John 5:11-12

I John 1:2

B. *From the Gospel of John.*

1. Turn to the third chapter of J o h n. The chapter records an interview between Christ, the master Soul-Winner and Nicodemus, a ruler of the Jews. From verses 1-2 it is clear that Nicodemus was not an atheist nor a skeptic. He believed in God, in miracles and he was sure that Jesus was a teacher come from God. But he saw Jesus only as a man, a man who had God *with* him. Nicodemus, a spiritually-blind Pharisee, could not see far in things spiritual because he was not yet born again. Therefore Jesus appraised the situation at once when He declared in verse 3, "Except a man be born again, he cannot *see* the kingdom of God." When Jesus said "a man" He was speaking of any

I Cor. 2:14

man, any member of the human race. Later when He said in verse 7, "Marvel not that I said unto *thee, ye* must be born again," He made the general application personal and specific. The "thee" was directed to Nicodemus and the plural pronoun "ye" applied to those whom Nicodemus represented. When Jesus said "cannot" He was simply affirming that it was impossible to see or enter the kingdom of God unless born again from above. When Jesus spoke of being born of "water and of the spirit" in verse 5, He was not speaking of baptismal regeneration. The apostle Paul declared that though he had only baptized a very few of the converts at Corinth, yet he testified that he had "begotten" them through the gospel. Millions can testify to the fact that they were born again and made new creatures in Christ Jesus when they put their trust in Jesus Christ Who was delivered for our offences and raised again from the dead for our justification.

1 Cor. 1:14-15
1 Cor. 4:15

2. Jesus went on to explain how the bewildered ruler of the Jews had or would have provision made for his salvation. Turn to verses 14-16 and point out that the death of Christ was necessary— "the Son of Man *must* be lifted up." Faith in Him alone brings eternal life to the soul. Emphasize the fact that Christ is *God's* gift, *God's* provision, *God's* way of saving a soul from death, eternal separation from God.

3. In bringing a soul to a definite decision, focus attention on verse 16. Make it personal, "God so loved *me* that He gave His only begotten Son for *me* that if *I* should believe in Him, I will not perish but have everlasting life." It is *God* Who gave. It is *we* who are to receive. The verse faces an individual with the necessity of reaching a verdict, accept or reject, take or refuse, believe or disbelieve.

C. *From the book of Isaiah.*

1. Use 53:6 and 64:6 to s h o w the n e e d for salvation.

2. Use 53:4-5 to p o i n t out the provision for salvation.

3. Then t u r n to 1:18 or 55:6-7 to show the enquirer the promise of salvation.

II. *Short sermons from monosyllables.*

Sometimes an opportunity to pluck ripe fruit is so apparent that one would be wise to use only one verse to point the soul to the Saviour.

1. Call. Rom. 10:13.

This verse has often been used most satisfactorily in dealing with souls who have come forward in an evangelistic service to accept Christ. In dealing with such, simply open the Bible to this verse and prayerfully and carefully emphasize each dominant word of the text. The verse lays down one condition of salvation, expressed in the use of the simple monosyllable "call." Obviously the call is a call of one in dire distress, the call of one who knows that he is lost, the call of one who knows that he must depend on Another to save him. It is clearly implied that it is a confident call and assurance is given that the call will be answered by the Lord Himself.

2. Turn. Ezek. 18:32.

I Thess. 1:9

Conversion involves a turning. It is turning *from* sin *to* Christ. It is turning *to* God *from* idols. A sinner bound and shackled by his sin, has only one hope of deliverance. It is not conversion to a church, a creed, a Christian or some cold code of conduct. It is conversion to *Christ.* Christ is God. He is God, the Son. In turning to *God* one receives enabling to turn *from* idols. Use this verse to show the seeker that in becoming a Christian, a change is imperative. An idol is anything that the heart prefers to God Himself. One must be prepared to turn from anything and everything that keeps one from loving God supremely and living for God solely. God will tolerate no rival.

Matt. 18:3

Matt. 22:37-38

3. Look. Is. 45:22.

This short simple monosyllable is sufficient to dissolve many hard problems encountered in dealing with one seeking salvation. Throughout life some have been busy

looking at the hypocrites in the church, looking at others
and looking at themselves but if one is to be saved,
he must look only to Jesus Christ. "Behold the Lamb
of God Who taketh away the sin of the world." One
must look to Christ for a very specific purpose—
John 1:29   "look unto me and be ye *saved*." One is to look to Christ
for salvation. It takes very little time to look. Just
Num. 21   as the smitten Israelites looked and lived and were
miraculously delivered from death when they did exactly
John 3:14-15   what God told them to do, no more and no less, so
the sinner in looking to Christ, is saved the moment
he trusts the Saviour.

4. Take. Rev. 22:17.

This word emphasizes the necessity of appropriation.
God has given: man is to receive. The sinner must reach
out and *take* by faith "the water of life freely." As water
is indispensable to life, so is Christ.

5. Come. Matt. 11:28.

While there is a sense in which the invitation of
Christ is extended to all, there is another sense in which
it is limited to those whose load of sin seems greater
than they can bear. Those who come unconvicted, go away
unconverted. When the weight of one's guilt crushes
a soul till it cries out to Christ for pardon and peace,
rest will be found. Use this passage in dealing with
one who is thus burdened and have him claim the
promise of peace.

III. *Follow-up work.*

Every new born babe in Christ needs a spiritual
I Cor. 4:15   mother. The high mortality rate among new converts
Gal. 4:19   is due to the neglect of the church in seeing to it that
every person brought to a saving knowledge of Christ
within her sphere of influence was not nourished and
I Pet. 2:2   cared for by some faithful follower of the Lord Jesus
Christ. The following suggestions are offered:

1. Obtain accurate information about his current
postal address and permanent home address.

2. See that some proper person visit, phone or write the new convert within forty-eight hours after his conversion.

3. Make sure that he is clear in the matter of the assurance of his salvation.

4. Show him the importance of meditation in the Word of God. Read the Word with him and suggest some simple method of Bible study. Ask questions. Answer his questions and get the person well grounded in the essentials of victorious Christian living.

5. Show him the importance of taking everything to God in prayer with thanksgiving, Phil. 4:6-7. Pray with him and encourage him to lead out in prayer.

6. Point out the importance of witnessing. Rom. 10:9-10.

7. Explain the necessity of Christian fellowship. Heb. 10:25. Take him to mid-week prayer meeting. Introduce him to other fellowships in the church that will help him to cultivate his spiritual graces.

8. Introduce the new convert to the Holy Spirit as:
   a. Teacher. John 14:26.
   b. Guide. Rom. 8:14.
   c. Fruit-bearer. Gal. 5:22-23.
   d. Intecessor and prayer-helper Rom. 8:26.
   e. Source of victory. Gal. 5:16; Rom. 8:1-11.
   f. Source of power for witnessing. Acts 1:8.

9. Train young converts to assume some responsibility in Christian service. I Thess. 1:9; Eph. 2:8-10; II Tim. 2:15.

10. No true Mother will forsake her child till assured that he is become a spiritual adult.

11. We deem it imperative that the new convert affiliate with some church immediately where he can be nourished with the milk and meat of the Word in the regular church service.

Examination on Lesson VIII

Marks	
5	1. Explain what is meant by "easy believism."
5	2. When would it be inappropriate to use Acts 16:31 in doing personal work?
5	3. Illustrate from Acts the part played by prayer in evangelism.
8	4. Give at least four ways of determining the reality of the new birth from I John.
10	5. Illustrate in what ways Jesus discouraged hasty discipleship.
15	6. Make clear how you will use Romans in dealing with a sincere seeker.
15	7. Make clear how you will use the gospel of John.
15	8. How might one use the book of Isaiah?
5 × 8	9. Quote and locate the five passages containing monosyllables on the way of salvation.
7	10. What are the first seven steps indicated in this lesson for follow-up work?
9	11. Where possible, locate Scripture for those steps.
24	12. How will you introduce the Holy Spirit to the new convert? Give Scripture references and in each case tell what the verse specifies concerning His work.
17	13. Quote Eph. 2:8-10 and explain how salvation and service stand related.

$$175 \times \frac{100}{175} = 100$$

LESSON IX

DEALING WITH THE CONFUSED

II Cor. 4:3-4

The devil is the author of confusion. By blinding the minds of those who believe not, he succeeds in keeping men in a dark and dismal dungeon looking for black cats that are not there. They call the cat an "excuse" and though they may be certain that the cat is a real cat, in reality it is only an illusion.

A study of the parable of the Great Supper in Luke 14:15-24 would justify the conclusion that an excuse is merely the skin of a reason stuffed with a lie. A man was giving invitations to a great supper. When all was ready, a servant was dispatched to call the guests. The first one spurned the call on the pretence that he had bought land and must immediately go to see it. Imagine a man buying land before he saw it and then having such urgency to view his newly acquired real estate that there was no other time to see it than the precise hour a sumptuous supper held in his honor, was being served! Surely the man must have been confused! The second one invited to the feast, had no better excuse. He averred having bought five yoke of oxen without having first proved them and then an irresistible urge had taken possession of him that necessitated his breaking a dinner engagement irrespective of the insult and injury done to those who had prepared the munificent meal. How ludicrous! What confusion! The third one invited to the supper confessed, "I have married a wife and therefore I cannot come." His excuse was conclusive. Marriage had disabled him. The others *would* not come: he *could* not. Many who *will* *not* come when invited to the gospel feast, may finally find that they *"cannot* come."

Prov. 1:24-33

Christ has prepared a *great* supper, sufficient for all. The gospel is a feast, not a funeral. Christ is the Bread

Isa. 55:1-2

John 6:35

Rev. 22:17

Luke 12:16-21

Gal. 1:4

Luke 14:21

II Tim. 2:24

James 4:13-14
Mark 8:36

Prov. 27:1
Prov. 29:1

John 4:20-24

II Tim. 2:13

Ps. 125:1

II Cor. 9:8

John 1:16

James 4:6

Prov. 3:5-6

of Life and "he that cometh to Him shall never hunger and he that believeth in Him shall never thirst." All down through the corridors of time, God's servants have been inviting guests to come, come, come. But men are too busy, too blind or too bound by their concerns for this life to stop, to see and to save themselves from this present evil world. Is it any wonder that the lord of the feast was "angry"?

However, God's servants should deal kindly and patiently with men's excuses. Some sincere souls are so utterly confused that they feel obligated to attend to the immediate without concern for the ultimate. But the urgency to come to the feast because "all things are *now* ready" is shunned and slighted for the most paltry pleas. The soul-winner must listen to men's excuses, diagnose them and then use the scriptures to lead any sincere seekers out of the prison of their confusion into the clear light of the gospel of Christ. Some of the excuses offered, are as follows:

I. *"I tried once and failed."*

In dealing with this excuse, which may be sincere or insincere, one may proceed as follows:

1. Create hope. The counsellor can joyfully and confidently assure such a person that many, including himself, have trusted in Christ and have made a success of the Christian life. Remind him of God's great faithfulness. Make it clear that while faith in ourselves is sure to issue in failure, faith in Jesus Christ will always bring blessing. Point out that the Lord provides abundance of grace, which is God's inward provision to meet every outward circumstance. But the Lord gives such grace to the humble, to those conscious of need and willing to acknowledge it.

2. Consider possible reasons for failure.

a. Trying instead of trusting. The whole secret of success in Christian living lies simply in trusting in Jesus for everything. To know the Lord is to trust Him.

Ps. 9:10
Matt. 6:25-34

When God is our Father and we are *His* children, we can trust and not be afraid.

Josh. 1:8
Ps. 1
Luke 10:41

b. The world instead of the Word. Failure to meditate daily in God's Word will result in failure. One can allow quite legitimate labor to crowd out the most important exercise of feeding the soul out of the treasury of the holy scriptures.

Prov. 28:13
I John 1:9
Ps. 32:1

c. Covering instead of confessing. God blesses the man whose sin is covered by atoning blood but He does not bless the one who covers his sin by refusing to acknowledge it and confess it to God. Where wrong is wrought toward another, confession and restitution

Matt. 5:23-24

must be made and reconciliation sought. Failure to fix a broken fellowship with a brother in Christ, failure to

Mark 11:25-26

forgive and forget, can lead to disaster. The best evidence that a Christian has been forgiven, is that he is willing

Eph. 4:32

to forgive others.

Luke 9:23

d. Self-assertion instead of self-denial. Determination to have one's own way is at the root of all sin. A person afflicted with "I" trouble will fail. The daily

Isa. 53:6

cross is much more than the bearing of the common

Rom. 7:14-24

trials of life. It is the renunciation of the self-life made possible through the recognition of the fact that our

Rom. 6:6

old man, our carnal nature has been crucified with Christ.

Heb. 6:17-20

3. Constrain them to begin again. Success in any realm does not come without the occasional failure. How-

Heb. 13:8

ever God cannot fail. Jesus is the same yesterday, today and forever. Entreat the one who would excuse himself by saying, "I tried once and failed" to trust the One Who cannot fail. Use the two passages appearing in the

Isa. 26:3-4

margin to encourage the timorous soul to put all his

Prov. 3:5-6

trust in the One Who is fully trustworthy.

II. *"I am waiting to make myself better."*

Some confused souls are persuaded that some degree of moral fitness is necessary before one can be saved. In dealing with such, trust the Holy Spirit to help you discern whether the person is sincere or insincere, wheth-

Eph. 2:8-9
Jer. 13:23
John 3:3
Isa. 64:6
Heb. 11:6
I Tim. 1:15
Luke 5:32

er the person is putting off salvation for other reasons or whether the enquirer considers salvation by grace too good to be true. If sincere, show him that no one can make himself better in God's sight any more than a leopard can change his spots. He *must* be born again. Outward reform is not sufficient if the heart remains unchanged. Show him that God requires faith, not moral fitness. Turn to a verse that shows that Christ Jesus came into the world to save sinners, not the righteous.

III. "The Christian life is too hard."

Prov. 13:15
Matt. 11:30
Heb. 11:25
Matt. 25:30
Ps. 16:11

Ps. 87:7
Jer. 2:13

II Cor. 5:11

To the contrary, it can be shown that the way of the transgressor is hard. Christ teaches us that His yoke is easy and His burden light. The pleasures of sin are only for a short season: the weeping and wailing in hell will be for all eternity. Fullness of joy is the portion of those who walk the path of life, the narrow way, in fellowship with Christ. Be sure, as a personal worker, that you are finding your own springs in God and not in the broken cisterns of this world or in its cesspools of iniquity. Joy that does not spring from a right relationship with God is shallow, superficial and short-lived. The Holy Spirit is full of strong desire to see men saved. Co-operate with Him by praying and pleading, working and witnessing, wooing and winning, visiting and revisiting till another soul is safe in the fold.

IV. "I can't give up my evil ways."

John 8:34
Rom. 5:6

Matt. 23:37
John 5:40

Luke 13:3

Agree with him and open your Bible to a verse that proves the truth of his assertion. Sin is a slavery from which Christ alone can set us free.

Ascertain whether his problem is "can't" or "won't." Paradoxical though it may seem, man is by nature both helpless and hopeless, and yet he is held responsible for the exercise of his will. He can choose or refuse. In choosing Christ, he will learn to thank Him alone for enabling him to choose and if he refuses, he will

John 6:65   be held accountable for not doing what God would have enabled him to do by His Spirit.

    Find out if the person making such an excuse is aware of where the broad road is leading. God requires Matt. 7:13-14   repentance.

    Emphasize the blood as the only ground of deliver- I Pet. 1:18-19   ance from the slavery of sin. By virtue of the precious Heb. 9:22   blood of Jesus, the problem is no longer, *"Can* you be free from your burden of sin?" but rather *"Will* you be free from your burden of sin? There's power in the blood."

Examination on Lesson IX

Marks

5	1. What does II Cor. 4:3, 4 teach us relative to the blindness of the minds of men who believe not the gospel?
3	2. What three excuses for not coming to the great supper are given in Luke 14:15-24?
10	3. Why was the Lord in the parable angry at the report of the servant? Think it through for yourself and offer at least five suggestions.
10	4. What analogies in this great supper do you find to the invitation to the gospel feast?
16	5. Quote and locate at least two appropriate passages of Scripture to use in creating hope in one who has tried and failed.
8	6. What possible reasons for failure are considered in this lesson?
4×8	7. Quote and locate at least one passage of Scripture to use in dealing with each of the suggested reasons for failure.
2×8	8. Quote and locate the two passages that one might use in constraining to begin again.
8	9. Quote and locate a passage that proves that salvation is by grace, not works.
8	10. Quote Jer. 13:23 and explain how it applies to the excuse of those trying to make themselves better.
8	11. Quote and locate the verse that proves that God requires faith, not moral fitness.
5	12. Quote I Tim. 1:15.
3	13. Where is the passage that proves that the Christian life is not too hard?
3	14. Where is the passage that shows that the pleasures of sin are only for a season?
3	15. Where does it say that Christ's yoke is easy and His burden light?
8	16. Quote John 8:34. How does this passage apply in this lesson?
8	17. Quote John 5:40. How does this passage apply?
12	18. Quote I Pet. 1:18, 19 and indicate how you intend to use this passage.
9	19. Quote and locate the passage that teaches that there is no release from sin without the shedding of blood.

$$\frac{175 \times 100}{175} = 100$$

LESSON X

DEALING WITH THE CONFUSED (Continued)

V. "I can't be a Christian in my present business."

I Cor. 7:20
Acts 18:3
Matt. 6:33

Find out what his business is. Some give this excuse because they imagine that being a Christian involves leaving a business life to engage in full-time gospel ministry. Make clear that the Lord does not call every man to leave his business, but simply to put God's business first.

Eph. 5:11
John 12:26

If a business cannot be conducted along Christian principles, then one must choose to get out of such crooked business and trust Christ with the consequences. God will not fail the one who honours Him. If the business is a God-honouring one and conducted according to Christian standards, then there should be no hesitation in clearing the business of every sinful or doubtful aspect.

Mark 1:18
Acts 4:4

Mark 8:36

Peter decided to leave his nets to follow the Lord. Later he won thousands of souls to the Saviour. Consider the loss to himself and to others if he had not made the right decision. When material prosperity is weighed in the scales of eternal values, what shall it profit a man if he gain the whole world and lose his own soul?

Let the counsellor work patiently with the man who thinks that he cannot be a Christian in his present business. The advice of another successful Christian business man might be sought on important matters.

VI. "If I go to hell, I will have lots of company."

Mark 9:43-48
Matt. 25:30, 41, 46
Luke 16:19-31

Find out if he believes in hell. Show him from the Word of God what hell is like.

From the standpoint of reason, the excuse offered reveals a very confused state of mind. Imagine the panic

on board a passenger plane plunging to the ground all
aflame! Does the companionship of loved ones and
friends on that plane lessen the distress? Will not companionship in hell aggravate rather than mitigate the
suffering? If the frown of a friend tipped the balance
of decision to reject Christ instead of receiving Him,
will fellowship with such a seducer in hell bring one bit
of comfort? No wonder there will be "gnashing of teeth"
in hell! No wonder the rich man became so mission-
ary-minded in hell that he pleaded with Abraham across
the impassable gulf, to send some one to warn his
brethren, lest they also come into that place of torment!
What insanity for respectable, religious people to *fear*
their friends more than they fear God and find themselves numbered with "the fearful" in the lake of fire
along with "the abominable and whoremongers"! One
cannot choose his friends in hell. One may let his friends
laugh him into hell but they will not laugh him out
again. Nothing so reveals the blindness of the human
heart and the devilish deception of the mind, than to
hear a person joke about perdition and say, "If I go to
hell, I will have lots of company." Sincerely but strongly
warn such to flee from the wrath to come.

VII. *"I am too great a sinner."*

Though religious and respectable, this was my own
excuse when approached about accepting Christ as personal Saviour. I was sincere but confused. It had never
occurred to me that Christ Jesus had come into the
world to save sinners, even the chief of sinners. The
conviction of the Spirit had been so deep and so real,
sin had been made so exceeding sinful in God's sight and
in my sight, that I was looking for the remedy, but was
held back by the thought, "I am too great a sinner."

Never tell such a person that he is not a sinner. Do
not even deny the possibility of his being a great sinner.
The problem is simply to show him that he is not *too*
great a sinner for *Jesus* to save. In speaking of sin
as *falling short* of the glory of God, it is important

Matt. 13:50
Luke 16:27-28

Rev. 21:8

Rev. 22:15

John 3:36
Matt. 3:7
I Thess. 1:10

I Tim. 1:15

Rom. 3:19

Rom. 3:23

Isa. 59:2

Eph. 4:24

for the counsellor as well as the enquirer to seek to apprehend the wideness of the gulf that separates man from God. As far as heaven is from hell, as much as sinful man is unlike a holy God, is the gap. As the hymn says, "O, the mighty gulf that God did span at Calvary!" Show the person that men "afar off" can be brought nigh by the blood of Christ. Direct the attention of the great sinner to the great Saviour by turning to such passages as Isa. 1:18; Heb. 7:25 or I John 1:7. Finish with a verse like John 6:37 that assures the one coming to Christ that he will in no wise be cast out.

Eph. 2:13

VIII. *"I'm afraid I've committed the unpardonable sin."*

Ask such a person what he considers the unpardonable sin to be. Some consider it to be murder. Another may think it is adultery. Wicked and wrong indeed are such sins but they are not the unpardonable sin. David committed both murder and adultery and yet his deep contrition and confession of sin brought assurance of divine forgiveness.

II Sam. 11

Ps. 32:5

Basically the unpardonable sin is unbelief. A man who *will not* believe cannot be saved. But there is a sense in which all men could be found guilty on this score and therefore if unbelief alone were the unpardonable sin, all men would be beyond redemption.

John 3:36

Rom. 11:32

When unbelief leads a man step by step to renounce and reject all light that God would graciously bring into a man's life, he may reach a point where he knowingly and deliberately blasphemes the Holy Spirit Who would lead him to Christ, regenerate him and seal him unto the day of redemption. There is a couplet which states it this way:

> There is a time, we know not when;
> There is a place, we know not where
> That seals the destiny of men
> For glory or despair.

From the account in Matt. 12:22-32, the unpardonable sin might be defined as an act which knowingly attributes to the Devil the work done by the Holy Spirit.

But the daring and deliberate accusation of the Pharisees who said, "This fellow doth not cast demons but by Beelzebub, the prince of the demons" was the climax to a course of unbelief. They did not believe that Jesus was the Son of the living God. They had rejected the witness of John the Baptist (Matt. 11:18). They had remained impenitent in spite of the attestation of His Messiahship by "mighty works" (11:20-24). They refused to respond to plaintive pleas to come to Him for rest and peace (11:25-30). They criticised and condemned Christ for doing good on the Sabbath (12:1-13). They held a council to determine how they might destroy Him (12:14). But Jesus withdrew, assured that in His name would the Gentiles trust (12:14-21).

This hardening of their hearts, this mounting opposition, this steeling of their wills against the light, reaches its apex in 12:22-37 where Jesus, in healing a demoniac who was both blind and dumb, is accused of performing this wonder by the power of Beelzebub, the prince of demons. That put the capstone on their unbelief. That was a deliberate insult to the Holy Spirit, in Whose power Jesus wrought His wonders. At that point they crossed a deadline and sealed their own eternal doom. Such people will have no desire to come to Christ. When the Holy Spirit withdraws, there is no drawing, no desire to come. It is not that God would not receive them, but simply that they have put themselves in such a condition of hardness, impenitence, and unbelief, that they have no inclination whatever to seek the Lord for salvation.

The person who manifests concern over the possibility of his having committed the unpardonable sin, is obviously not one who has committed such sin. Ask the enquirer if he considers that he has followed such a course of unbelief. Enquire if he has persistently refused to admit that Jesus was the Son of God in spite of abundant attestation to His deity. Find out if he has climaxed his open antagonism to the Son of God by attributing some specific sign of His divinity to Satan. Assure him, that if he had, he would not be worrying over his action. Turn to a promise like John 6:37 and entreat him to come to the Saviour without delay. Warn him of the danger of drifting, departing, degenerating and finally despising and denouncing the divine Deliverer. Do not pass out pleasing platitudes to a careless procrastinator. "He that being often reproved, hardeneth his neck, shall suddenly be destroyed and that without remedy."

Prov. 29:1

IX. *Other excuses, briefly considered and answered with Scripture.*

1. "I don't believe the Bible." John 7:17; I John 5:9-12; Mark 16:16; II Tim. 3:16-17.

2. "I am doing the best I can." Isa. 64:6; Eph. 2:8-9; Tit. 3:5.

3. "I would rather not do it now." II Cor. 6:2; Heb. 2:3.

4. "I could never keep it up." I Pet. 1:5; Jude 24.

5. "My problems are too difficult." II Cor. 12:9-10; Matt. 19:26; Phil. 4:13.

6. "I have been seeking Christ but cannot find Him." Jer. 29:13; Luke 19:10; John 1:12.

7. "I cannot forgive a person who has done me a great wrong." Mark 11:25; James 4:6.

Examination on Lesson X

Marks

30 1. Make clear how you will proceed in dealing with one who imagines he cannot be a Christian in his business. Quote and locate at least three appropriate Scriptures to use in such an inquiry.

30 2. Do the same in explaining how to deal with one who says, "If I go to hell I will have lots of company."

30 3. How will you deal with one who says, "I am too great a sinner"?

6 4. On what ground do you believe that neither murder nor adultery are the unpardonable sin.

5 5. Basically, what is the unpardonable sin? Explain.

15 6. By the use of your Bible for this question only, point out from the context of Matt 12:31-32, what course in unbelief leads ultimately to the deliberate rejection of light and salvation?

 7. Quote and locate Scripture to use in dealing with each of the following excuses:

8 a. "I don't believe the Bible."
8 b. "I am doing the best I can."
8 c. "I would rather not do it now."
8 d. "I could never keep it up."
8 e. "My problems are too difficult."
8 f. "I have been seeking Christ but cannot find Him."
8 g. "I cannot forgive a person who has done me a great wrong."

$$175 \times \frac{100}{175} = 100$$

LESSON XI

DEALING WITH THE CARELESS

Ps. 142:4

The reason why there are so many careless sinners is because there are so many careless saints. The history of great revivals proves that an awakened church will inevitably result in the reaching of those who carry little or no concern for their spiritual welfare.

Mark 16:15

Luke 14:21

Mark 16:20

Ps. 126:6

Gal. 6:9

Mark 8:36

I Pet. 1:18-19

Ezek. 3:17-19

Since we are commissioned to preach the gospel to every creature, the careless are not to be shunned and neglected. The church must go forth into the highways, the homes, the hovels and even sometimes into the haunts of sin to rescue the perishing. "He that goeth forth (not he that sits at home) and weepeth, bearing precious seed, shall doubtless come again with rejoicing bringing his sheaves with him." It will take a great deal of prayer, patience and perseverance to win some of these people to the Saviour. But a Christian awakened to the worth of a soul, aware of the colossal cost of his redemption, will most gladly spend and be spent for their salvation.

Acts 20:31

Luke 12:47

Jonah 2-3

Acts 26:19

I Cor. 11:31

We are God's watchmen. While the world sleeps on amidst the darkness of impending judgment and doom, Christians must get out their gospel trumpets, warn men to flee from the wrath to come and win them to faith in the Christ of salvation. The Christian church will be held responsible for the unsaved of their generation who go into the flames of an eternal hell with no word of warning from us, no word of gospel light, no prayers, no tears. Let Jonah repent and Nineveh will repent. Let the church repent of her disobedience to Christ's clear commission, let her shoulder the blame for the surging stormy seas in the world, let her confess to the world that she has not been obedient to the heavenly vision, let her judge herself if she would escape being judged, then the world will hear and heed. If it is midnight, a man may not appreciate being roused from his stupor and his sleep, but when he makes the discovery that his home is on fire, he will thank the one who sounded out the alarm. It is criminal negligence to let people perish when we know that their life is about to be consumed.

In dealing with this class, one may never get an opportunity to say very much at any one given time, yet a word in season, when spoken in the Spirit, may be the first link in a chain that will eventually lead to his salvation. Since we are to warn every man and teach every man "in all wisdom" one may use scripture to show the careless that he is:

Col. 1:28

I. *Lost.* Luke 15; Luke 19:10; II Cor. 4:3-4.

Luke 15 presents three parables revealing the state of the lost and the story of an individual's salvation. The parable of the lost sheep directs our attention to the concern of the shepherd for the one among a hundred. The dire need of that one sheep drew the attention of the shepherd away from the ninety and nine, who are not left in the shelter of the fold, as we so fondly sing, but "in the wilderness." The ninety and nine are representatives of the proud Pharisees who complained about Jesus receiving sinners and even eating with them. The one is very obviously the poor publican who knows that he is lost.

Ps. 119:176

Luke 15:4

Luke 15:2-3

The Bible teaches that sinners are like sheep. They go astray when they go their own individual way. Ignorant of the dangers, defenseless against the devouring beasts, they suddenly awaken to their lost estate. Their lamentable and plaintive plea is heard by the seeking shepherd and he brings that one sheep only into the shelter of home. Christ is the Shepherd. Men are the sheep. But there is a difference between the one sheep and the ninety-nine. The one was lost and found. The others were left in the wild wilderness among the wolves. A careless sheep will be forsaken: the lost sheep will be found. For every seeking sinner there is a seeking Saviour. Entreat the careless soul to picture himself as that one

Isa. 53:6

John 1:11

Matt. 23:37

Luke 19:1-10

sheep who wandered from the shepherd who is right now seeking for him. Christ listens for his cry. There will be joy in heaven over one sinner repenting. There will be no joy over the ninety-nine who imagine that they did not need to repent.

Luke 15:7

Luke 13:3

Men are not only like lost sheep. They are like the lost silver. Does the silver know that it is lost? Neither do some careless souls. But the woman cared and she got a light and a broom and swept the house till she found the precious silver. Some souls are lost within the shelter of the church or religion. A little house-cleaning in the light of the Spirit and the Word may lead to the recovery of souls lost within the walls of the church. The seeking of lost souls is the work of the church as well as Christ. In this ministry, we are to be labourers together with Him. But while ninety-nine out of a hundred may be lost in the wilderness, nine out of ten may be lost right inside the nominal church.

II Cor. 6:1-2

Rev. 18:4

Rev. 3:1-2

The prodigal son wilfully set his face toward the far country. Worldly wealth has led many men and nations to turn away from the father's house to seek pleasure in riotous living. Not until all is spent and a soul is forced to cry out, "I perish!" will there be any inclination to return. Sometimes the soul-winner has to wait long years for the return of the prodigal but go on waiting —patiently, prayerfully, expectantly. Have the "fatted" calf ready for his return. God can dry up all his springs, bring such famine as will blast all his fortune, and so engineer all the circumstances that he will have to admit, "I went out full and the Lord has brought me home again empty." The parable reveals the utter insanity of sin, the sovereignty of God, the responsibility of man, the inexpressible joy attendant upon the sinner's determination to forsake the far country to minister for ever in the father's house. The elder son, who pouted and complained at the grace shown to the younger son, is very typical of many respectable religionists who remain outside the door and angrily refuse to go in.

Isa. 2:7-8

Hosea 4:7

Luke 15:13

Luke 15:17

Ruth 1:21

Luke 15:18

II. *Guilty.* Rom. 3:19.

Most men will admit that they are sinners in some

Rom. 3:9

Rom. 1:32

Rom. 2:16

degree at least, but few have ever been made to realize that they are *guilty* sinners. They are guilty before *God*. In the epistle of Paul to the Romans, he proves from reason, revelation and observation that all men are guilty and under sentence of death. What an awakening this should produce in the careless who imagines that he can stand in the judgment before the gaze of a glorious God Who knows what he *is* and knows *all* that he has done.

III. *Condemned.* John 3:18; 3:36.

Once a soul has been found guilty, the judge must pass sentence in keeping with the law. The world is guilty. They are condemned *already*. The sentence of death has been passed. But there is a judicial ground on which God can freely justify the sinner. That ground has been established by the highest authority in the whole wide world, by God Himself. By His grace, through the blood of Christ, a condemned sinner may find justification. How? Through faith in the blood of His Son to remit and forgive our sin, giving us a right to stand before Him, clothed in His righteousness, as though we had never sinned. To trample that blood under our feet, to despise it, to disregard it, to deplore it, is to expose one's soul to God's righteous wrath.

Rom. 8:33
Rom. 3:24
Rom. 5:1, 9
Rom. 3:25
Rom. 8:1
Heb. 10:29

Heb. 10:31

IV. *Hell-bound.* Rev. 21:8; Matt. 25:46.

Shallow views concerning the enormity of sin and the essential holiness of God have caused many to tone down the teaching of the Word of God regarding the final consequences of continuing to live carelessly. Some people are careless because they fear what their friends will say. They fear their scorn, their frowns, their ridicule, the loss of their fellowship. This may be put first in the list in Rev. 21:8 because it constitutes by far the largest class. But how solemn the thought that millions will weep and wail in hell forever because they feared the face of a man that would die and feared not God

Matt. 25:30
Matt. 13:50

Acts 4:12

Who liveth and abideth forever, the same holy and righteous God Who can not save any man apart from His Son.

If death is the common lot of all men, then there is no point to the plaintive plea of the prophet, "Why *will* ye die?" If physical death alone is the wages of sin, then salvation is meaningless, Christ died in vain, moral distinctions are needless and the suffering of the righteous in this world avails nothing. God would neither be holy, righteous or loving and His Word would be a lie if there is not somewhere down the future a time when there will be a final separation of the evil and the good, the wicked and the righteous. The same book that describes the glories of heaven, speaks also of the horrors of hell. Just as truly as God says, "The righteous shall go into life eternal," He says also, that others "shall go away into everlasting punishment." There would be no reason for continuing the punishment of one that had long since ceased to exist. The Bible does not teach the annihilation of the wicked. It does teach the eternal punishment of the wicked.

Ezek. 18:31

Matt. 13:30, 41

Matt. 13:49-50

Rev. 21-22

Rev. 14:10-11

Matt. 25:46

It is our responsibility to warn tearfully, to care compassionately, to go forth to rescue the perishing and to throw out the life line to men sinking in the sea of sin. When travelling into the Peace River country in Alberta, Canada, the train stopped at McLennan. It was early in the morning. While talking to a man on the station platform, I noticed smoke issuing from a basement hotel window just opposite the depot. On running into the hotel, it could be seen that the whole basement was an inferno. Scores of people were asleep in that hotel. I saw their danger: they were blissfully ignorant of the impending doom. The alarm was given. The guests were aroused, the rooms checked and cleared and in the matter of ten minutes the building was empty of all personnel. Was it wrong to excite those guests at such an hour? Did any one stop to argue as to whether I was telling the truth? Did it matter what religion, what race or what relation they were to me? The only thing that mattered was to exonerate myself of all blame for negligence in seeing that all, old or young, friend or foe, were delivered from the flames. If some careless characters had gone back to sleep after being duly warned, they could not have blamed the faithful few who cried "Fire! Fire!" To have just remained where they were, would have meant to perish.

Examination on Lesson XI

Marks	
3	1. Where in the Bible does it say, "No man cared for my soul"?
6	2. Why are we not to neglect the careless? Two references.
7	3. Quote Gal. 6:9 and explain how it stands related to this lesson.
5	4. What solemn warning is given in Luke 12:47 to those who know the Lord's will and refuse to do it?
10	5. How did Jonah stand related to Nineveh's need? What did Jonah do when first commissioned? What did he do later? How is Jonah like the Church?
3	6. Where in the Bible are we told to warn every man and teach every man "in all wisdom"?
10	7. What two classes of people did Jesus have in mind when he gave us the three parables in Luke 15? Where did the shepherd leave the ninety-nine? Whom do they represent? Are there any people who do not need to repent? Why? How are men like sheep?
10	8. Why are men like lost silver? Whom does the woman represent? What may the house represent? Who is responsible for losing the silver and who is responsible for finding it? What must be done before she finds it?
6	9. What Bible illustration can you give to show that nations as well as individual families and individuals often go to the far country away from God when tested by prosperity?
4	10. Make clear from the parable of the prodigal son that God holds men responsible for their decision to return.
10	11. Quote Rom. 3:19. Make clear how you intend to use this verse in dealing with a careless character.
10	12. Quote John 3:18 and 3:36.
12	13. Who justifies? On what ground may a person be justified? Through what may a man be justified? Give Scripture references or quotations for each of these.
10	14. Quote Rev. 21:8 and Matt. 25:46.
4	15. Why are there such shallow views about eternal punishment?
15	16. Give at least five reasons why you believe that the wages of sin is much more than mere physical death.

$$\frac{125 \times 100}{125} = 100$$

LESSON XII

DEALING WITH THE CARNAL

Carnal Christians within the church do more harm to the cause of Christ than do the ungodly outside the church. When babes in Christ remain babies, when born-again believers fail to grow in grace and in the knowledge of their Lord and Saviour Jesus Christ, when Christians walk after the flesh instead of the Spirit, the church has a prodigious problem on her hands. It is a deadly disease. It is a progressive plague that will spread like an epidemic. It is a malignant cancer that weakens its victim till it renders him helpless.

Carnal Christians will giggle their way out of assuming any responsibility to reach the lost. They pray little and care less. They know the hockey stars but they do not know the Holy Spirit. They know the rules of the football game but they are ignorant of the laws and principles that govern successful spiritual living. They love the world: they speak of the world: they go to the world for their entertainment and enjoyment because they have forsaken the fountain of living waters and hewed for themselves cisterns, broken cisterns, that can hold no water.

Jer. 2:13

Even evangelical churches are reeking with this malady. It has been so subversive and so subtle that the average pastor will consider that I am looking through dark glasses. But the shores of time are strewn with the wrecks of those who have drifted in from the seas of lust and passion and not a few of these have been men and women who once occupied prominent places in church circles.

Some may refer to such as "backsliders" and that may be a fair designation. But inasmuch as the term "backslider" is not used in the New Testament, permit me to cut a wide swath that will include the person who has very definitely turned back from following the

91

Lord and the person who manifests *inclinations* to pursue the same course. Carnality leads to backsliding and backsliding begins with some form of carnality. The carnality may be intentional or unintentional. But it severs the soul from that fellowship with Christ which is essential to growth. If sin can be nipped in the bud, it will never have a chance to bring forth its obnoxious fruit.

Jas. 1:14-15

In dealing with this class, one should diagnose the cause, determine the consequences and discern the cure.

I. *The cause.*

1. Drifting. Heb. 2:1-4.

Heb. 3:1

Heb. 10:32-35

The epistle to the Hebrews is addressed to Hebrew Christians. At one time they had suffered much for the gospel, had taken joyfully the spoiling of their goods because of the assurance that they had "in *heaven* a better and an enduring substance." But the rugged road of discipleship was seemingly beyond their endurance. They had stopped "going on" and in stopping they had started to drift with the current. They had drifted to the point where they were back in a state of spiritual infancy. They were carnal. They were backslidden. Therefore the epistle furnishes the church with a strong exhortation to press on toward the goal, while at the same time warning all who would fail to press on, of the dangers ahead.

Heb. 12:6-13

Heb. 6:1

Heb. 5:12-14

Heb. 12:1-3

Heb. 10:38

A carnal Christian drifts away from the Lord when he hears but does not heed the Word of God (2:1). The further one drifts with the current of carnality, the fainter grows the voice and the more heedless the response to divine direction. Such negligence, if continued, is dangerous. How shall any man escape if he drifts away from God, despises His Word, disobeys His commands and dishonors "so great salvation"? It is not a question of *rejecting* salvation. It is *neglecting* to work out that salvation in daily living.

Heb. 2:2

Heb. 2:3

Phil. 2:13

Tit. 2:11-12

The grace of God that brings salvation teaches a man to deny ungodliness and worldly lusts and to live soberly, righteously and godly *in this present world.* The writer asks a question that even God cannot answer and he includes himself when he asks, "How shall *we* escape if *we* neglect so great salvation?" There is no need for trying to water down the seriousness of the warning here. Entreat a carnal Christian to beware of the drift, to hear and heed the Word of God and to work out his own salvation with fear and trembling, knowing that it is God Who worketh in us both to will and to do of His good pleasure.

2. Disbelieving. Heb. 3:7-19.

Drifting beyond the sound of His voice provides Satan with a golden opportunity to fill the mind with doubt and unbelief. Unbelief kills enthusiasm and makes people content to mope about in a waste howling wilderness for years when through faith they might have entered Canaan, the land of milk and honey, "of brooks and water, of fountains and depths that spring out of valleys and hills; a land of wheat and barley and vines and fig trees and pomegranates; a land of olive and honey; a land where thou mayest eat bread without scarceness, thou shalt not lack anything in it." The writer of Hebrews warns, "Take heed, *brethren,* lest there be in any of *you* an evil heart of unbelief in *departing* from the living God."

Num. 14:1-12

Deut. 8:7-9

Heb. 3:12

3. Degenerating. Heb. 5:11-14.

Christians who drift toward unbelief, can soon degenerate, become sluggish, slothful and spiritually dwarfed and finally reach a condition where *it is impossible* to renew them again unto repentance. God's Word can minister to any man in strict accordance with his particular need at the time. A man adrift, heedless and careless, wicked and worldly, needs warning, not comfort. If salvation past, is not salvation present, it may not be salvation future. The emphasis in the Bible is not on salvation from hell, but salvation from *sin* which makes hell necessary for those who persist in the practice of sin.

Heb. 6:4-8

Matt. 1:21

Tit. 2:14

Rev. 22:11

4. Despising. Heb. 10:26-31.

A Christian who does not find delight in the Word
may end up despising it. Even the infinite sacrifice
of Christ can be little appreciated and the precious blood
of Jesus can be dangerously deprecated. Some have
followed such a course. To anyone, Calvinist or Armi-
nian, saved or unsaved, let there come the solemn warning, do not despise the precious blood of Christ shed
for the remission of your sins.

5. Departing. Heb. 12:25-27.

This final warning from the book of Hebrews is
intended to draw attention to the danger of turning
away from Him Who speaks with such power and authority that His voice will one day occasion the very dis-
solution of the heavens and the earth. How foolish to
live for this passing world when God has called us
to live for a world that can never pass away! And so the
drift away from the Word of God in Heb 2:1-4, the
hardening of the heart in refusing to heed His Word
in 3:7-8, can cause degeneration, lack of appreciation
for Christ's sacrifice on Calvary and final departure.
Constant neglect of the Word is fatal to faith.

II. *The consequences.*

1. Discouragement. Jer. 2:25.

Jeremiah, who wrote his prophecy particularly for the
backslider, teaches that backsliding leads to discouragement. Their language is, "There is no hope." This is
the most used weapon of Satan. Jesus is never discouraged
and He can never fail. People get discouraged when
they fail to pray and put their help upon the One Who
is mighty. "We should never be discouraged. Take it to
the Lord in prayer." And is not prayerlessness the product
of carnality? A carnal man considers himself self-suf-
ficient. He has enough personality to win friends and
influence people to follow him and he has never been
put into such a state of utter helplessness that God alone
could be his Help. When a man knows God intimately,

Jer. 2:25

Isa. 42:4

Ps. 62

Acts 27:25

he can sing in the storm, "He *only* is my Rock and my salvation." Such a soul will not be discouraged.

2. Defilement. Jer. 2:7.

II Cor. 6:14-18
Haggai 2:13

Jas. 1:27

Jude 23
Exod. 33:3
Deut. 1:42
Num. 14:42
Hos. 5:6

When a Christian neglects fellowship with God, he seeks his fellowship with the ungodly. Thus he is defiled, unfit for use in God's service and an unclean soul infects every thing it touches. James exhorts believers to keep their garments unspotted from the world. Jude admonishes believers to *hate* even the garment spotted by the flesh. God will not dwell in the midst of a people who will refuse to separate from the world. God withdraws His conscious presence from the disobedient, the obstinate and the worldly. If the church as the Bride of Christ refuses to keep her garments clean, she renders herself unfit for His company. The church that cannot lift up "holy hands" in prayer, is carnal and backslidden.

I Tim. 2:8

Ps. 24:3-5

The Christian who goes to worship with unclean hands and an impure heart, cannot receive "the blessing." Some people who go to church to worship and sing with hands and heart defiled would do well to obey the injunction of practical James who wrote, "Draw nigh to God and he will draw nigh to you. Cleanse your hands ye sinners; and purify your hearts, ye doubleminded. Be

Jas. 4:8-9

afflicted and mourn, and weep: let your laughter be turned to mourning and your joy to heaviness. Humble yourselves in the sight of God and He will lift you up."

3. Deceit. Jer. 8:5.

Jeremiah said of Judah, "They hold fast deceit." Judah did not turn from religion when they backslid. They had their priests, prophets and pastors. But they determined they were going to govern the kind of preaching they would hear. They hated Jeremiah because he refused to itch their ears with smooth-feathered words. God is seeking worshippers who will worship *Him* in the Spirit and in *truth*. A backslider who holds fast deceit, deceives only himself. Even the world detects this hollow mockery and looks with scorn upon such hypocrisy.

4. Despair. Jer. 2:19.

Backsliding leads to despair. The prodigal son went

into the far country when he was rich but he turned
his face toward the Father's house when he was about
to perish with hunger. Jonah discovered that a course
in disobedience led only to despair. Consider the desperate straits into which God had to bring that evangelist before he prayed in earnest. If a disobedient child
of God is without chastisement, he is a bastard son.

Heb. 12:8

III. *The cure.*

1. Repent. Ps. 51; Rev. 2:5, 16, 22; 3:3, 19.

In real repentance there will be contrition for sin.
The Hebrew word for "repent," *nacham* in the Old Testament, denotes such shades of meaning as, to rue, to
regret, to moan, to groan, to mourn, to grieve over, to
feel regret, to repent so as to produce a change of conduct or purpose. God-given repentance will bring deep
remorse and such genuine sorrow for sin that it is most
unlikely that it will ever have to be repeated. When the
carnal Corinthian fornicator was in the pangs of sorrow
for his sin, Paul was concerned lest he be swallowed
up with grief. But that was real repentance that did not
require repetition.

II Cor. 2:7

Some look disdainfully upon David because of his
sin. Truly it was grievous and inexcusable but let his
critics listen attentively as he sobs out his confession in
Ps. 51. David repented and David left us the record
of the infinite mercy of a pardoning God when a sinning
saint will humble himself in genuine repentance. The
Bible is not written to reveal the virtues of humanity:
it unfolds the greatness of God's grace to the undeserving.
It points the penitent to a cleansing fountain where the
blood cleanses from *all* sin. Five of the seven churches
in Revelation 2-3 are commanded to repent. Impenitence
for sin is the bane of the modern church. This must precede confession.

I John 1:7

2. Confess. Prov. 28:13; I John 1:9.

To confess sin is to go along with God in adopting
His attitude toward it. God hates sin: so must we. Sin

separates men from God, men from men, Christians from Christians.

Ps. 51:4

Ps. 32:5

Lev. 6:2-5

Luke 19:8

Matt. 5:24-26

Since sin is basically an act of transgression against God, it must be confessed to God. However, when one is convicted of specific acts of transgression against men, he must also confess to those whom he has wronged. A satisfactory settlement will have to be made for such wrongs. To be right with God will necessitate obedience to God in the matter of restitution of goods, restoration of fellowship and the righting of any wrongs within the range of possibility.

3. Claim the promise. Jer. 3:12, 22.

Jer. 3:14

Jer. 3:1

Isa. 55:7

I John 1:9

God is married to the backslider. Assure the one returning to the Lord that God looks and longs for his return, that He will abundantly pardon, that He will cleanse from *all* unrighteousness and sin.

Examination on Lesson XII

Marks

10   1. Using the introductory notes of this chapter as a starting point, write your own description of a carnal or backslidden Christian.

5
10
15   2. What five causes of backsliding do you observe in Hebrews? In each case give the reference and in each case explain how the practice of the failure leads further and further away from God.

10   3. Quote Tit. 2:11, 12.

6   4. Give at least three reasons why you believe the book of Hebrews is addressed to Christians.

15   5. Point out the inconsistency of sin in a Christian in the light of Matt. 1:21; Tit. 2:14 and Rev. 22:11.

35   6. Quote Heb. 10:26-31. According to this passage and its context, what is the willful sin for which such stern warning is given here?

2
5   7. What is the first consequence of backsliding according to this study? How do you account for this effect?

2
10   8. What is the second consequence of backsliding? Use Scripture references with appropriate comments to show the seriousness of such a course in life.

2
5   9. What is the third consequence? Show how this sin affected Judah according to the prophecy of Jeremiah.

2
4   10. What is the fourth consequence? Illustrate from Scripture.

6   11. What three steps are indicated in the cure?

5   12. Express what is implied in repentance.

2
5   13. Where in the Bible do you read of David's repentance? Indicate at lease five features of his repentance.

10   14. Quote Prov. 28:13 and I John 1:9.

10   15. Explain fully what is implied in making full confession.

24   16. What assurance can be given to a carnal backslider if he will thoroughly repent and return to the Lord? Quote and locate at least three passages.

$$200 \times \frac{100}{200} = 100$$

LESSON XIII

DEALING WITH COMMUNISTS

Preparation for dealing with Communists involves education and dedication before there can be effective evangelization.

I. *Education.*

One who is to deal effectively with Communists must first of all understand Communism and its aims.

Dr. Fred Schwarz, of Sydney, Australia, perhaps the most competent exponent of the Communistic philosophy, says in his book, *The Heart, Mind and Soul of Communism* (The Christian Anti-Communism Crusade, Box 508, Waterloo, Iowa), pp. 7-9:

> Communism is a religion of promise. It has advanced across the world on the wings of promise. The promise is twofold in nature. . . . One aspect appeals to the poor . . .; the other appeals to the wealthy, the intellectually superior and the idealistic reformers. . . .
>
> To the poor . . . the servants of Communism go with this message: "Follow me, and I will build a new world for you and your children, a world from which hunger and cold have been forever banished; a world in which war and pestilence are mere historic memories, a world without exploitation of man by man, a world without racial animosity and discrimination, a world of peace and plenty, a world of culture and intellect, a world of brotherhood, liberty and justice."
>
> . . . to seduce the rich . . . to enlist the educated . . . to ensnare the idealistic . . . they say that not only is there to be a new society created, but there is also to emerge a new and finer mankind. Human nature is to be transformed into something infi-

nitely finer and more beautiful. Mankind is to be redeemed from vice, depravity and sin in all its forms.

To the question, how do they expect to bring this to pass, the Communist has one word: "Science." Scientific Marxism set forth three basic hypotheses for their scientific program, (a) Atheism, (b) Materialism, (c) Economic Determinism. Karl Marx was an atheist before he was a Communist. His greatest disciple, Lenin, said, "Atheism is a fundamental portion of Marxism, of the theory and practice of scientific socialism" (Ibid., p. 13). Their materialistic philosophy of life declares that man is matter in motion and nothing more, . . . man is an animal and nothing more, that the whole realm of existence can be explained on the basis of evolutionary sequence. With reference to economic determinism, Dr. Schwarz explains it this way (Ibid., pp. 15, 16):

> The entire personality, including thoughts, emotions, religious experiences, family attitudes, sentiments, and artistry is derived from the prevailing mode of economic production. We are the captive creations of the Capitalistic system. It has ordained what we shall think, how we shall feel, and what we shall do in any given situation. The Communist Manifesto makes this lucidly plain. It specifically states that the family as we know it, the hallowed relationship of parent and child, is derived from the Capitalistic Economic System and that parental love will vanish with the vanishing of Capitalism. It goes further and specifically states that the concepts of freedom and justice are derivatives of the class struggle, and that when class struggle ceases, the concepts will disappear. No one is individually responsible for his character or thoughts. As his class of social origin has determined, so he thinks, feels and acts. To change character and personality what is needed is a basic change in the economic system.
>
> It follows logically that all undesirable human characteristics are derived from the prevailing economic system. Communists are realists. They affirm the depravity of human nature; everywhere

men and women are lazy, ignorant, self-indulgent, patriotic, and religious—no one could build a Communistic social order from such poor raw material. The first essential is a radical program aimed at the root cause of human depravity—the Capitalistic Economic System and a consequent program to purify and perfect mankind. This must be done in a scientific manner. The inescapable sequence of scientific steps is as follows,

1. Destruction of the Capitalistic System, the root of all evil by a violent revolution.

2. Institution of the Dictatorship of the Proletariat.

3. Liquidation of those classes of society incurably diseased by Capitalism and considered dangerously infective.

4. Segregation of those diseased but capable of useful work in conditions of isolation.

5. Hospitalization of the diseased but curable in "corrective" labor camps.

6. Re-education of the total population in new relationships of labor with the emphasis on labor rather than reward.

7. The emergence of the young generation with characteristics uninfluenced by Capitalism and appropriate to a socialist environment.

8. The perfection of the human race.

9. The withering away of the State; the Dictatorship of the Proletariat.

10. The emergence of Communism.

By a process of infiltration into governments, churches, sporting bodies, industrial labor unions, etc., the Communists work toward the fomenting of a revolution in which a minority can take over control of a vast majority. For example, in 1949, 7,000 Communists in Australia came close to the conquest of 8,000,000 people by armed assault without any outside support.

Communists regard the liquidation of the Capitalistic classes as simply scientific animal husbandry—an infectious herd to be destroyed without sentiment and simply in obedience to scientific principle. They hold that their mass-murder program is science in action. Their heartless cruelties are not to be attributed to the barbarous instincts of any particular peoples or race, but simply to their scientific philosophy that if a disease is incurable, the victim must die. Even the word "murder" is to them a "bourgeois" term. The killing of the diseased is simply cold, inexorable, scientific logic.

Inasmuch as Communists regard America as being a country where the disease is more rampant, American Communists estimate that over fifty millions will have to be liquidated in America. The putting of millions into labor camps is regarded as a quarantine, to keep them from infecting others. The average time taken for such to die, is three years. The slave-labor camps are regarded by Communists as "personality hospitals," and they boast, "hospitalization is free."

Gradually the golden age of Communism arrives, in which every one works for the sheer joy of working, where men the world over are brothers. The slogan of this period is, "From every man according to his ability; to every man according to his need." But as Dr. Schwarz points out (*Idem.*, p. 26):

> Every fact of Communist history contradicts the specious optimism that human nature will perfect itself under the dictatorship of the Proletariat. The evidence provided against this thesis provided by the Communists themselves is shattering. Take the deterioration that has taken place in the character of leading Communists under the Russian system. In 1917 the Central Committee consisted of 31 members and alternates. . . .

> Lenin and Sverdlov died before Stalin came to power, Alexandra Kollontai lived to die a natural death. The remainder degenerated into such offal, such swine, such treacherous wild beasts, such hyenas—using Communist terminology—that every one had to be put to death. When Lenin died in 1924, the Politbureau, the highest body of World Communism, had seven members—Zinoviev, Kamenev, Stalin, Bukharin, Trotsky, Rykov,

and Tomsky. All but Stalin degenerated and had to be destroyed (of course, Stalin is dead now also). The perfection of character is thus revealed as a delusion.

II. *Dedication.*

If Christians would dedicate themselves as fully to Christ, as Communists do to Communism, the cause of Christ would not be in jeopardy. Let us compare the two philosophies of life.

1. Discipleship.

The true Communist lives his life in utter obedience to the mind and will of the Party. At its slightest wish he will lie, cheat, or kill; he will inflict or suffer the most intense torture; the individual is nought, the Party is all.

Phil. 1:21
Rom. 12:1
Mark 10:29-30
I John 2:3-6

To a Christian, Christ is all. His body is presented as a living sacrifice. Family, friends, finances, fame and fortune are all to take second place. Submission to Christ and obedience to Him, is to be the normal life of every child of God.

To a nominal Christian who spoke of going to the movies, a Communist replied, "Yes, the movies. I used to like them very much, but since I joined the Communist Party two years ago, I have been so busy studying Philosophy, attending meetings and distributing literature that I have never had time to go to the movies once." [Dr. Fred Schwarz, *The Christian Answer to Communism* (Great Commission Press; Anderson, Indiana), p. 26.]

2. Study.

II Tim. 2:15
II Pet. 3:18

Every Communist is a student.
Every Christian should be a student.

3. Stewardship.

Dr. Schwarz gives this illustration of the devotion of a Communist in the stewardship of his time and money (*Idem.*, p. 28):

A known Communist was met by an acquaintance in San Francisco and was asked where he was going. He replied that he was going to a meeting. "What! at midnight," came the surprised reply, "there won't be anyone there." "Have no doubt about it; everyone who should be there will be there. One third of my day I work; one third of my day I sleep and attend to personal needs. One third of my day I give to Communism. Half of my income I give to the Party."

Should a Christian be any less devoted to Christ in the light of Gal. 2:20; 6:14; I John 2:15-17?

III. *Evangelization.*

If the principles set forth in previous lessons in this course had been diligently followed by every child of God, Communism would never have gotten started. Dr. Schwarz suggests (*Idem.*, p. 29):

> The Christian forces opposing Communism must be organized and disciplined. Organization is no substitute for life but it provides the engine within which the gasoline of conviction, consecration and courage may move the mountain of lethargy, self-indulgence and ignorance which provide the inflammable debris through which the Communist Party is consuming the earth. The organization must be dedicated to truth, not unity. It must be an organization of like-minded, clear-sighted, self-renouncing Bible-believing Christians who can channel their corporate energies into definite goals. A Unit of Theological Contradictions and Ecclesiastical Opposites in a programme of the lowest common denominator of faith and action such as that represented by the World Council of Churches or the United Nations is a parody of the true Christian organization needed desperately to combat Communism. Organization, like fire, is a good servant but a bad master. Such an organization of consecrated Christians must be built and fired by the Spirit of God in this tremendous battle.

Communism thrives among unregenerate men because it feeds the flames of man's innate enmity toward God

Rom. 1:28-32
Eph. 2:2
Rom. 3:10-18
Rom. 5:10

I Tim. 4:1-3
Ps. 14:1-2
Rom. 3:18
II Cor. 4:3-4
Eph. 6:17
Ps. 119:130
Heb. 4:12

Rom. 1:16

I Thess. 2

Rom. 3:20-31

I Cor. 6:20
James 2:15-17
1 John 3:14-18
Col. 1:16
John 1:9
John 4:24
Rom. 2:15
I Thess. 5:3
Matt. 10:21-22

and will do so as long as the usurper Satan, the prince and god of this world, is allowed to rule men's lives. Communism is the philosophy of the natural man because it gives expression to that which lies coiled up in the bosom of a depraved heart. Show the Communist that his philosophy of life is accurately described in the Scriptures. If a Communist can stab or stifle his conscience to the point where he avows that there is no God, then one should not be surprised to find that there is no fear of God before his eyes. Living in the dark, he cannot see. Blinded by the god of this world, he cannot see. Against this hellish darkness, the servant of God must employ the Word of God. The entrance of God's Word will give light.

The Word of God is living and powerful and it is sharper than any two-edged sword. The fearless proclamation of the gospel of God's grace is our best answer to Communism. That gospel must thoroughly transform us before we can effectively preach it. Flowing like a crystal stream from the lips of a holy man of God, full of the almighty Spirit of God, the philosophy of atheistic Communism must wither and die. If one is allowed to open the scriptures to show the parallels between what the Bible teaches on human depravity and what Communism practices and teaches, then one may proceed to show that the same Bible which analyses the disease of sin, also prescribes a cure.

Though it does not fall within the compass of this course to deal in detail with their false tenets, it can be confidently declared that Communism is pseudo-science. Its evolutionary philosophy has been proved to have not one single scientific prop on which to rest. Its political science has been demonstrated to be equally impractical and impossible. If Communists are brothers, then the Christian concept of brotherhood has lost every semblance of its significance. Its materialistic philosophy of life contradicts the conscience, the conduct of men all through history and is a flat contradiction of the truth of the Scriptures. It promises peace but gives none. Its most ardent defenders must live in constant jeopardy

John 14:27

Micah 4:1-4

Isa. 9:7

II Cor. 5:18-21

Rom. 1:18, 32

Rev. 13

II Thess. 2:1, 8-9

Dan. 2:44

of their lives. Any deviation may mean liquidation.

In contrast to this, it can be pointed out that Christ does give peace. Millions have proved it to be so. The Christian knows that some day peace will reign when the Prince of peace takes the government of this world upon His shoulder. Show the Communist that God is reconciled to man in the death of Jesus Christ. Beseech him to be reconciled to God. God waits for man to lay down his enmity toward Him. To ignore God is to invite His wrath and they that do such things are worthy of death and damnation. At the close of this age, when a Dictator, the Antichrist, will endeavor to liquidate the righteous from off the face of the earth, the Lord will return, destroy the Antichrist, deliver His people and establish a kingdom that never will be destroyed.

Examination on Lesson XIII

Marks	
2	1. What does preparation for dealing with Communists involve?
2	2. Who is a competent exponent of Communistic philosophy and what is the name of the book he has written explaining the nature of Communism?
6	3. What two-fold promise does Communism make to the poor and to the rich?
2	4. How does the Communist propose to bring utopia?
3	5. What three basic hypotheses constitute the scientific program?
5	6. Who was Karl Marx' greatest disciple and what did he say with respect to God and scientific socialism?
5	7. What is man according to Communism?
10	8. What is meant by economic determinism in the Communistic philosophy according to Dr. Schwarz?
5	9. What does the Communist hold with respect to human depravity?
10	10. What sequence of scientific steps does Communism propose to follow in establishing their philosophy in a country?
5	11. Illustrate how a minority of revolutionists may take over control of a vast majority.
5	12. What is their attitude toward liquidation of masses?
5	13. Explain what they mean by "personality hospitals"?
5	14. How can it be proved that the perfection of character under Communism is a delusion?
6	15. Compare the Communist and Christian attitude toward discipleship.
20	16. Quote and locate Scripture to show what is involved in Christian discipleship?
5	17. Why is a Christian to *study* according to II Tim. 2:15?
5	18. Illustrate stewardship as it pertains to a Communist.
5	19. How do you explain the phenomenal growth of Communism? (In 38 years they have increased their membership from 40,000 to over 800,000,000).
10	20. How can it be proved that Communism is pseudo-science?
5	21. How does Matt. 10:21-22 relate to Communism?
10	22. What does Christian brotherhood mean?
14	23. How is peace to be established?

$$\frac{150 \times 100 = 100}{150}$$

LESSON XIV

DEALING WITH CATHOLICS

The exhortation of Paul to Timothy in II Tim. 2:24-26, is very urgent for any one who would achieve success in winning Catholics to Christ. The servant of the Lord must be gentle, able to teach, patient and meek as he instructs with a view to recovering them from the snare of the devil, to whom they are captive slaves. To Protestants who know the historical record of Rome's intolerance down through the course of the centuries and the truth about bloody brutalities practiced on evangelicals in lands dominated by Rome in this modern era, the imperative of Paul to the servant of the Lord that he "must not strive" looks ludicrous. Nevertheless it stands written, "Preach the word; be instant in season, out of season; reprove, rebuke, exhort with *all longsuffering* and doctrine" II Tim. 4:2. A Christian is completely cast upon Christ Who is full of grace as well as truth. Christ *in* us is sufficient.

I. *Deal wisely.* Matt. 10:16; James 1:5; 3:17; Dan. 12:3.

In sending His disciples forth as sheep into the midst of wolves, our Lord's first admonition was, "Be wise!" Wisdom comes from God and He has a liberal supply available to those who pray and depend upon Him for it. That wisdom, James says, is "pure, then peaceable, gentle, and easy to be entreated, full of mercy and good fruits, without partiality and without hypocrisy." The problems met in dealing with Roman Catholics in a country dominantly Protestant, are vastly different to those met in areas where Rome is supreme. Personal work is never a mechanical matter. There are Catholics who have little use for their church, no respect for the priesthood, no confidence in the Pope nor his cardinals. There are others who are fanatical in their fury to harm, kill and destroy. Study your patient before prescribing a cure. Diagnose each individual case and discern, in deep dependence upon God for wisdom, just how to approach that person.

II. *Deal intelligently.* Matt. 28:19; II Tim. 2:24-25.

One must learn before he can teach. The servant of the Lord must be "apt to teach" and capable of "instructing those that oppose themselves." Therefore one should know Catholic doctrine and be able to point out its inconsistencies, showing that their own Bible opposes the basic tenets of their faith. If it can be shown that their doctrines are contradicted by their own Bibles, then their clamorous claims to infallibility, apostolicity, unity and universality, are exploded. Let us examine a few of their claims:

1. Peter and the Pope.

They teach that Peter was the first Bishop of Rome, the rock on which Christ would build His church, that he was ordained of God to have primacy over all the earth; that to Peter were given the keys of the kingdom of heaven with authority to open or shut the door of heaven to men, to bind or loose souls from the effects of their sin; that this authority has been transmitted from Pope to Pope in one unbroken succession.

We reply:

a. There is not one text in the Roman Catholic Bible to prove that Peter was ever the Bishop of Rome. If so, he was absolutely ignored by Paul in his epistle to the Romans. Yet Paul sent special salutations to many at Rome. In fact, Peter was the particular apostle to the circumcision. Peter wrote his first epistle from Babylon, to Christians scattered throughout Asia Minor. There is no mention of Rome in his second epistle and he was near death at that time.

b. The Greek word for Peter, *Petros,* signifies "a

Rom. 16

Gal. 2:7

I Pet. 1:1,
5:13

II Pet. 1:14

stone." The word used for Rock, when referring to Christ, is *Petra*. Did Christ explicitly say in Matt. 16:18 that He would build the church upon Peter? The Roman Catholic Bible does *not* say so. Neither Peter nor the other apostles so interpreted the declaration of Christ. Paul did say that Christ was the foundation of the church. Paul did say that Jesus Christ was "the chief corner stone," and that the household of God was built upon the foundation of "the apostles and prophets" and not upon any particular apostle or prophet—implying the teaching of both the Old and New Testament Scriptures. Peter himself referred to Christ as headstone and Christ at one time called Peter a "stumbling-stone."

I Cor. 10:4

I Cor. 3:11

Eph. 2:20

I Pet. 2:7

Matt. 16:23

c. Peter made no claim to primacy over all the earth. Authority in heaven and earth is Christ's prerogative to the end of this age. Much to the contrary, Peter taught submission to governmental authority. He never admonished any one, "Submit to me!" but enjoined his fellow-elders to feed the flock and not to act as some lord over *God's* heritage but to practice submission to one another in genuine humility. Paul made it plain that Christ is the Head over all things "not only in *this world* but also in *that which is to come*" (Eph. 1:19-23).

Matt. 28:18-20

I Pet. 2:13-17

I Pet. 5:1-6

d. It is wrong to assume that Christ gave Peter authority to open or shut the door of heaven to men. Christ is *the* Door to salvation and the promise is, "By *me* if *any man* shall enter, he shall be saved and shall go in and out and find pasture." Moreover the authority to bind and to loose, spoken to Peter in Matt. 16:19, is available to any believer who will learn to pray effectually. Apostolic authority is delegated authority, not individual or personal authority. For example, when Peter preached on the day of Pentecost, "Repent and be baptized every one of you *in the name of Jesus Christ* for the remission of sins," he was using *delegated* authority. Later, on healing the impotent man, he explained, "Why look ye so earnestly on us, as though by *our own power* or holiness we had made this man to walk? The God of Abraham . . . . hath glorified His Son Jesus . . . . and *His name* through *faith in His name* hath made this man

Matt. 16:19

John 10:9

Matt. 18:18-20

strong" (Acts 3:12-16). Likewise in preaching to Gentiles, Peter explained, "To him (Christ) give all the prophets witness that through *His name* whosoever believeth in *Him* shall receive remission of sins."

Acts 10:43

Peter rested the authority for faith for the remission of sins upon the testimony of the entire Old Testament scriptures (all the prophets), who in turn prophesied of Christ of Whom the New Testament also bears witness. The Scriptures are the testimony of God. They are of divine authority. There is no higher authority than God's authority. Christ, being God, has power to forgive sins. Any believer may come to Christ and claim this authority from the scriptures written by prophets and apostles. Therefore when a believer declares in this twentieth century, "My sins are forgiven," he does not need to seek the sanction of the Roman church nor its priesthood. He has divine authority from the Word of God, of which the writers of the Old and New Testament scriptures were but the instruments to make known the good news.

John 1:6-7

John 17:8, 14, 17

II Tim. 3:16

Mark 2:5-12

Acts 10:43
I John 1:9
I John 5:13

Eph. 1:7
Col. 1:14

Isa. 1:18

Isa. 44:22
Ps. 32:1
Ps. 103:1-2
Ps. 103:12

e. It is wrong to speak of Peter as the first Bishop and that the Roman Catholic church was the first church. The first church was in Jerusalem from which place the gospel spread to all the civilized earth (Acts 1:8). When dissension arose over circumcision, a conference to decide the issue was called for at *Jerusalem* (Acts 15:2).

Until the beginning of the fourth century, the blood of untold multitudes of Christians washed the streets of pagan Rome. Then with the conversion of Constantine, he threw open the doors of the church to pagans who had never been born again. What some historians call the greatest hour of Christianity, was really its darkest hour. The pagan priests brought their ritual into the Christian church. Instead of worshipping their female deities, they substituted the worship of another woman, Mary. There was no such thing as the Roman Catholic hierarchy for the first 400 years of the Christian church. When Constantine wedded the church to paganism, there began to emerge as offspring of this wicked union, prayers for the dead, worship of angels and saints, the mass (A.D. 1100), enforced celibacy of priests (1123), sale of indulgences (1190), transubstantiation of the wafer (1215), auricular confession of sins to the priest (1215), purgatory proclaimed (1438), immaculate conception of Mary (1854), infallibility of the Pope (1870), the Assumption of Mary (1950).

2. Mary.

They teach that Mary is the mother of God; that she is the great Mediatrix between God and men; that she is the Door to heaven; that she is the keeper of souls; that prayer is to be addressed to Mary; that she was sinless; that she was taken up bodily into heaven without dying.

We reply:

a. If Mary were the mother of God she would be before God and God would not be eternal. In this assertion, the Roman Catholics blindly contradict themselves. Catholics will look in vain for one Scripture to prove that Jesus ever referred to Mary as his Mother. He addressed her as "Woman." Jesus was "the seed of the woman" as to His human nature, but He was Emmanuel, "God with us." As God, He was before all things.

b. The Roman Catholic Bible says, "For there is one God, and *one* Mediator between God and men, himself man, Christ Jesus" (I Tim. 2:5). Then what right does the Roman church have to put Mary in the place of Christ? There is only *one* Mediator, not two. How can Rome be regarded as an infallible teacher when she contradicts the scriptures of her own church?

c. To say that Mary is the Door to heaven is flatly contradicted by the Roman Catholic Bible in John 10:9.

d. Not Mary, but Christ is the Keeper of souls. Mary failed to keep her own son in Jerusalem.

e. No apostle or saint of the New Testament prayed to Mary. Prayer is to be addressed to the Father in the name of the Son.

f. Mary spoke of God as "my Saviour." If she had not been a sinner she would not have needed a Saviour.

g. If Mary ascended bodily into heaven, why did it take nineteen centuries to make the discovery?

John 2:4
John 19:26

Gen. 3:15

Matt. 1:28

Col. 1:17

II Tim. 1:12
Luke 2:42-49

John 15:16

Luke 1:47

In Acts 1:14 Mary is mentioned for the last time. The letters of the apostles ignore her. Christ alone is our Advocate and Intercessor (I John 2:1-2). The rich man in Luke 16 prayed to Abraham, but even such a saint as Abraham could not help. In Luke 11:27-28 Jesus put the Word of God before His mother and rebuked the one who praised her. In Matt. 12:46-50 Jesus completely ignores His mother's request.

Examination on Lesson XIV

Marks

25   1. Quote II Tim. 2:24-26 and II Tim. 4:2. Make clear the importance of the application of the exhortation in dealing with Catholics.

15   2. Quote Matt. 10:16 and James 3:17 and show how they apply.

5   3. In dealing intelligently with Catholics what must one be able to do?

5   4. Name at least five things taught by Roman Catholicism concerning Peter and the Pope.

30   5. By the use of Scripture references refute each of the five tenets you have referred to in question 4.

6   6. Name at least six things taught by the Roman Catholic Church about Mary.

36   7. By the use of Scripture references refute each of the six points you have referred to in question 6.

15   8. Quote Luke 11:27-28 and explain how it applies.

8   9. Point out how the conversion of Constantine was really the darkest hour of the church.

5   10. Give at least five dates for the birth of new Roman Catholic dogmas down through the course of the centuries.

$$150 \times \frac{100}{150} = 100$$

LESSON XV

DEALING WITH CATHOLICS (Continued)

3. Mass and Communion.

The Roman Catholic Church teaches that "The Mass is the unbloody sacrifice of the body and blood of Jesus Christ. It is the same sacrifice as that of the cross because it is the same offering and the same priest, our Lord Jesus Christ" (Catholic Catechism). They teach that the wafer in the hands of a priest is changed into the real body of Christ (transubstantiation). The Masses are to be spoken in Latin. There are high Masses and low Masses. In a high Mass, they light more candles, use more incense, have more music and the service lasts longer. They pay more for a high Mass than a low Mass.

The fabrication of this doctrine of the Mass was approximately the year 1100. The transubstantiation of the wafer became Catholic doctrine about 1215. The denial of the cup to laymen came in 1415. The word "Mass" comes from the Latin participle "Missa" which is the feminine form of the perfect participle of the verb *mitto,* meaning "to send." It suggests the idea of forgiveness, that is, the *sending* away of sin. Is there any scriptural support for their doctrine in the Catholic Bible?

We reply:

a. In Heb. 10:11-12 it reads as follows, "And every priest indeed stands daily ministering and often offering the same sacrifice which *can never take away sins.* But Jesus, having offered *one* sacrifice for sins, has taken his seat forever at the right hand of God. For by *one offering* he has perfected *forever* those who are sanctified. Now where there is forgiveness of these, *there is no longer offering for sin."* So, according to the Roman Catholic Bible, Jesus offered Himself, the one and only sacrifice needed to put away sin.

117

b. Transubstantiation contradicts the plain teaching of the apostles. Paul, in referring to the institution of the Lord's supper in I Cor. 11:23-34, spoke of the bread as bread after His giving of thanks. At the institution of the Supper recorded in Matt. 26:26-30, Christ referred to the wine as "the fruit of the vine" and not as blood. The Catholic theologians allow for a distinction between the sign and that which is "sign-ified." When Jesus took bread there was a distinction between the bread and His body. He did not give them His body to eat but He gave them bread which represented His body. The cup did not contain His blood for that was not shed till He died on the cursed tree. Moreover the miracles of Christ never contradicted the senses. They were attested by the senses. Can any Roman Catholic communicant say that the eating of the wafer is identical to eating raw human flesh?

c. Two elements are concerned in this Sacrament—bread and wine. In the early church both elements were taken by the communicants (I Cor. 11:23-26). The command of Christ to eat the bread was as emphatic as the one to drink the wine (Matt. 26:27). Who gave the Catholic church authority to contradict the teaching of Christ in saying that the wine is for the priest only?

d. To speak in Latin, in a tongue unknown to the common Catholic is, according to the Catholic Bible in I Cor. 14:9, to act like a barbarian or a raw heathen.

Eph. 1:7
Col. 1:14
Col. 2:13

John 1:29
I John 2:2
Rom. 6:23
John 3:16
I John 5:12

e. Show a Roman Catholic from his own Bible that forgiveness of sins is the precious possession and privilege of the one who trusts in Christ alone. Jesus Christ is the Lamb of God Who took away the sin of the world. The sin question was settled at Calvary. The Son question is, "What will you do with Jesus?"

4. Purgatory.

They teach that purgatory is the state or place in which the souls of the faithful, after death, are purified from venial sins in purgatorial fires and thus made ready for heaven; that the sufferings of souls in purgatory after death can be lessened by sacrifices, imposed by the

Catholic church on the living; that the Pope has power to bind or release such souls when satisfied that the uttermost farthing has been paid.

We reply:

a. There is not one verse in the Catholic Bible about purgatory.

b. It could be pointed out however that *if one is a child of God,* to die is "to depart and to be with Christ . . . far the better" (Phil. 1:23). "Exiled from the body . . . at home with the Lord" (II Cor. 5:8). The plain, unmistakable teaching of this Roman Catholic Bible is, that the moment we leave this body, we are in the presence of the Lord.

c. Judgment for a Christian's sins is past. Let me read it to you in this precious Roman Catholic Bible, "Amen, amen, I say to you, he who hears my word, and believes him who sent me, has life everlasting, and does not come to judgment, but has passed from death to life" (John 5:24). The thief on the cross went directly to be with Christ in paradise, not purgatory. The blood of Christ alone purges from sin, not our sufferings. Nothing you can pay can get your loved ones out of purgatory fire for, since purgatory does not exist, they are not there.

Luke 23:43

5. Baptism.

They teach that "baptism is a sacrament that cleanses from original sin, makes us Christians and children of God and heirs to the kingdom of heaven" (Butler's Catholic Catechism). To the question, "Does baptism also remit the actual sins committed before it?" they reply, "Yes, and all the punishment due to them." They teach that unbaptized babies go to Limbo if they die and will never see God or be in heaven.

We reply:

John 3:16-18

a. John 1:12-13 and Gal. 3:26 teach that one becomes a child of God by receiving Christ, trusting in Him to save us from perishing and giving us everlasting life. It is the blood of Christ, not water, that washes

I John 1:7

I Cor. 4:15
I Cor. 1:14-16
Luke 23:43
Luke 19:9
Acts 11:14-17
away our sin. The Corinthian Christians were born
again, not by water baptism, but by the gospel of Christ.
The thief on the cross was saved but he was not bap-
tized. Zacchaeus was saved but not baptized. Cornelius
was saved before he was baptized.

  b. There is not a syllable in the Roman Catholic Bible about Limbo. It is often used by the Church to extort
money. Appealing to the strong sentiments of mothers,
Roman Catholic priests have threatened to refuse to baptize the babies born to Catholics if they deviate from
their loyalties to the mother church. No Catholic mother
need live under this reign of terror. Jesus said, "Suffer
the little children to come unto me and forbid them
not: for of such is the kingdom of heaven." Of the baby
born to Bathsheba and died, David said, "I shall go to
him." David expected to go to the same place that the
baby went and David did not go to any Catholic Limbo.

Matt. 19:14
II Sam. 12:23

  6. Celibacy.

  In 1123 the Roman Church came out with a new
dogma, the celibacy of the priesthood. Is there any support in the Catholic Bible for this practice? None whatever!

  a. Heb. 13:4 says, "Marriage is honourable to all."

  b. I Cor. 9:5-6 says, "Have we not power to lead
about a sister, a wife, as well as other Apostles, and as
the brethren of the Lord, and Cephas (Peter)."

  c. I Tim. 3:2 says, "A bishop . . . must be the husband of one wife."

  7. Mixed marriages.

  In the Roman Catholic book entitled *The Question
Box,* by Priest B. L. Conway, of the Paulist Fathers, with
the Imprimatur of Archbishop Farley and containing a
preface written by Cardinal Gibbons, on page 509, is
the following statement on mixed marriages: "The Catholic Church grants a dispensation from the ecclesiastical
law forbidding mixed marriages, because she hopes in
certain peculiar cases that these evils may be obviated.
She lays down three conditions: 1st, Both parties must

promise that all the children be reared in the Catholic faith. 2nd, The non-Catholic must promise not to interfere in any way with the religious life of the Catholic. 3rd, The Catholic must promise to do everything possible by prayer, good example and persuasion to bring the non-Catholic to the true faith."

If any Christian takes such a pledge before a Roman Catholic priest, he has not only deliberately disobeyed the Scriptural injunction, "Be not unequally yoked together with unbelievers" but he has publicly denied Christ and declared himself an apostate. To put your light out is to put yourself in the darkness.

II Cor. 6:14

Matt. 10:33

Since, to a Catholic, marriage is a sacrament that can be dispensed only by the Church, Protestant marriages are not valid, in their opinion. Disregarding the laws of the land (Canada), Roman Catholic priests have remarried Catholics married to Protestants by a Protestant minister and have made the parties submit to the vows expressed above.

III. *Deal patiently.*

The servant of the Lord *must* not only be wise and intelligent in his dealing but he must be patient and purposeful. A soul, steeped in the superstitions and slavish fears of the Roman Catholic Church, must be won by prayerful and persistent effort. Jesus commanded us to go and *teach* all nations. It is much more difficult to teach truth to one indoctrinated with error. But one must meet the authoritarianism of this false church with the "Thus saith the Lord" of the Scriptures. While doctrinally, she professes to be the defender of the faith and the originator of the truth found in the Bible, in practice she has kept her people in ignorance of the scriptures and has been the cruel opponent of the Word of God.

The best ally of Roman Catholicism has been an apathetic Protestantism. Our icy indifference may cost us the loss of our liberties. Our sin is the sin of silence. The Christian is to be aggressive, militant, active. The

command to "Go and teach" is not a challenge. Disobedience to this plain command is the cancer of the
church. But a revival would not only cure the church of
this disease but it would save millions of Catholics from
the disaster of an endless eternity in the fire that never
shall be quenched.

Examination on Lesson XV

Marks	
5	1. What does the Roman Catholic Church teach regarding the Mass?
2	2. What is meant by transubstantiation?
2	3. Distinguish between a high Mass and a low Mass.
6	4. When was this doctrine fabricated and how was it developed?
5	5. How does Heb. 10:10-12 contradict the teaching of the Mass?
10	6. Make clear that the teaching of transubstantiation is unscriptural and unreasonable.
4	7. Point out from the Scriptures that communion involves the partaking of two elements.
5	8. Why is it wrong to use an unknown tongue in the church?
24	9. Quote and locate three passages which prove that forgiveness of sin is a present possession of the believer.
6	10. What three principles do they teach about purgatory?
16	11. Quote and locate two Scriptures to show what happens to a child of God at death.
8	12. Prove that judgment for a Christian's sins are past.
5	13. What do they teach about baptism?
20	14. Give at least five Scriptural proofs that baptism does not save.
10	15. Why do we reject their teaching about Limbo?
12	16. Give three references to prove that the celibacy of the priesthood is unscriptural.
6	17. What three promises must a Protestant make in marrying a Catholic?
6	18. How serious a matter is it for a Christian to make such vows?
8	19. Discuss the need of employing patience in dealing with Catholics.

$$\frac{160 \times 100}{160} = 100$$

Summary of Part II

In dealing with any class or condition of men, depend upon the Word of God and the Spirit of God to effect the miracle of the new birth. Salvation involves a radical change. It brings to a soul a revelation of both the holiness and the love of God. Seek earnestly but tenderly to lead men to Christ. He is the Saviour. Some people get converted to a church or to an evangelist who never get converted to the Lord Jesus Christ. Use only enough Scripture to clear the understanding of the seeker as to what is involved in the decision. But be sure to visit or keep in touch with every one professing conversion till they are out of spiritual infancy and able to digest solid food. Keep in mind that any true conversion involves two things, repentance toward God and faith toward our Lord Jesus Christ. Make clear to the one starting out on life's new way that keeping company with Jesus through prayer and Bible study and constant abiding in Him is the way to live abundantly. Encourage the new convert to witness and win others to Jesus Christ.

PART III

PRESENTATION OF THE FAITH VERSUS CULTS

LESSON XVI

"JEHOVAH'S WITNESSES"

I. *History.*

Charles Taze Russell, born 1852 in Pittsburgh, was the founder of the movement now known as "Jehovah's Witnesses." At an early age he rejected the doctrine of eternal torment and entered upon a long and varied career of denunciation aimed at "Organized Religions." In 1870, at the age of 18, Russell organized a Bible class in Pittsburgh and in 1876 they elected him "Pastor" of the group. In 1879 Russell founded "Zion's Watch Tower" which is known today as "The Watchtower Announcing Jehovah's Kingdom." This magazine now (1956) has a circulation approximating 2 million per month. His chief work was *"Studies in the Scriptures,"* which was published in seven volumes from 1881 to 1917. As of July, 1956, "The Watch Tower Bible and Tract Society" has known branches in over 63 lands, and missionary work in over 104. The Society now owns a large printing establishment, a modern apartment building and office quarters, a radio station and a Bible School that has sent out over 1,000 missionaries.

(When a Baptist pastor in Hamilton, Ontario, published a pamphlet exposing the self-styled "Pastor" Russell as a fraud and denounced Russell's whole system as "anti-rational, anti-scientific, anti-Biblical, anti-Christian and a deplorable perversion of the gospel of God's dear Son" Russell sued Ross for "defamatory libel." Russell lost the suit and was convicted as a perjurer. If any one wants proof of the dishonesty of Russell, his lack of morals and unfitness to "pastor" any people, the story is on file in the Police Court at Hamilton, Ontario, Dec. 9, 1912 and Feb. 7, 1913; also in the files of the High Court of Ontario—Russell vs. Ross—"defamatory libel," March, 1913.)

Upon the death of Russell in 1916, the Society was taken over by Joseph Franklin Rutherford, who had been Russell's attorney. He was never a judge even as Russell was never a pastor. He conceived the idea of making each member of the movement believe himself to be one of Jehovah's final witnesses to the nations and so the movement became known as "Jehovah's Witnesses." Under his leadership the work spread rapidly. He produced over 100 books and pamphlets, which were in turn translated into many different languages. He died in 1944.

The new president is Nathan H. Knorr. He founded the Gilead Missionary Training School in South Lansing, New York, and held the International Convention of "Jehovah's Witnesses" in Yankee Stadium, New York, in the Summer of 1953.

II. *Name.*

Their name, "Jehovah's Witnesses" is supposed to have its Scriptural sanction in Isa. 43:10-12. That the name, as applied to this cult, is inappropriate, is proved as follows:

1. The words, "Ye are my witnesses" in 43:10 were originally addressed to Israel (43:1).

2. The New Testament teaches us to be witnesses unto *Christ* (Acts 1:8); witnesses unto His resurrection (Acts 1:22; 2:32; 3:15); witnesses of His death and resurrection which alone make possible forgiveness of sins (Acts 5:30-32; 10:39-43). But the "Jehovah's Witnesses" virtually deny the physical resurrection of Jesus Christ—which identifies them as "false witnesses" (I Cor. 15:15). The New Testament teaches us that a true witness has the Son of God, has eternal life and knows that he has eternal life on the basis of the record that God has given us of His Son (I John 5:10-13). The New Testament teaches us that the Holy Spirit bears witness with our spirit that we *are* the children of God. Those who have received Christ are the only ones who have any right to witness for Jehovah (Rom. 8:16-17; John 1:12).

3. The One speaking in Isa. 43:10-12 is the LORD or Jehovah God. That He is identical with the Lord Jesus Christ, is proved as follows:

a. The LORD is Creator, Isa. 43:1, 7, 15; and so is Christ, John 1:1-3; Col. 1:16; Heb. 1:1-3.

b. The LORD is Redeemer, Isa. 43:14; and so is Christ, I Pet. 1:18-19.

c. The LORD is the only Saviour, Isa. 43:11; and so is Christ, Acts 4:12.

d. The LORD is the first and the last, Isa. 44:6; and so is Christ, Rev. 1:8.

e. The LORD is God, Isa. 43:12; and so is Christ, John 1:1; Matt. 1:23; Rom. 9:5; Tit. 2:13; I John 5:20.

f. The LORD is our Shepherd, Ps. 23:1; and so is Christ, John 10; I Pet. 5:4; Heb. 13:20.

g. The LORD is our Healer, Exod. 15:26; and so is Christ as abundantly proved in the Gospels and such passages as James 5:15.

h. The LORD is our Righteousness, Jer. 23:6; and so is Christ, I Cor. 1:30. And so one might go on *ad infinitum.* Thus in denying the deity of Christ, their name is a pseudonym.

III. *Their Doctrines.*

1. The Person of Christ.

They teach:

a. Christ was created. They base their assumption on a misinterpretation of Col. 1:15 and Rev. 3:14. J. F. Rutherford, in *Harp of God,* p. 98, says, "The Logos was the first and only direct creation of Jehovah."

b. Christ never was and never will be God. J. F. Rutherford, in his book *The Truth Shall Make You Free,* says, "He is *a* mighty God but not the Almighty God who is Jehovah."

c. Christ was only a man while upon earth and died as a man. C. T. Russell in *Studies in the Scriptures,*

Vol. V, and page 453 declares, "The man Jesus is dead, forever dead."

d. Christ was originally a created angel, known as "Michael, the archangel." C. T. Russell in *Studies in the Scriptures,* Vol. V, p. 84, says, "As chief of the angels, next to the Father, He was known as the archangel, whose name, Michael, signifies God's representative." And J. F. Rutherford agrees with this when he says, "In this office (begotten Son of God and first-born of every creature) he bore another name in heaven, which name is Michael. It means, 'Who is like God.' " See *The Truth Shall Make You Free,* p. 49.

We reply to each of these false tenets:

a. Christ was not created: He is the Creator of *all* things (Col. 1:16). To insert the word "other" before "things" as they do in their New World Translation of this passage, has no foundation whatever. This is a clear example of "Handling the Word of God deceitfully." Christ cannot be a creature and at the same time the Creator of *all* things, including angels. The expression "firstborn" in Col. 1:15 is to be understood in the light of Col. 1:17, "the first-born from the dead." And this is not to say that Christ was the first to be *raised* from the dead but He was the first to rise from the dead in His resurrection body, the "firstfruits" from the dead, the pledge of the resurrection of all who are united to Christ by faith. "Christ, being raised from the dead, dieth no more; death hath no more dominion over Him."

Christ's resurrection body is the pattern to which all redeemed and resurrected bodies will be conformed. It is a perversion of the Scriptures to read "first-*born*" as though it were "first-*created.*" Concerning His incarnation the prophet Isaiah said, "A child is *born*" but of His eternal Sonship, he said, "A Son is given."

The Hebrew word for God in Gen. 1:1, *Elohim,* allows for a multiplicity of persons taking part in the first creative act but the use of the singular verb, *bara,* points to the unity of the action. The triune God are shown by other scriptures to have taken part in the crea-

II Cor. 4:2

I Cor. 15:21

Rom. 6:9

Phil. 3:20

Isa. 9:6

tion. When John speaks of Christ in Rev. 3:14 as "The beginning of the creation of God" he is saying something which is in full agreement with what he has said in the gospel of John in 1:1-3, where he avers that Christ was *with* God in the beginning and that He, the *Logos*, was God. "In the beginning *God* created the heaven and the earth." To speak of Christ as the first creature that God created is to put meaning that is not there. It is eisegesis, not exegesis.

b. Christ was, is and ever will be God. This is proved by the fact that

(1) He has divine names. Isa. 9:6; Matt. 1:23; John 1:1.

(2) He is worshipped. Matt. 2:11; 14:33; 28:9; Luke 24:52; Heb. 1:6; Phil. 2:10-11; Rev. 5:8. It is idolatry to worship any one but God (Exod. 20:4-5). Peter knew that it was wrong for a mere man to accept worship (Acts 10:25-26). Paul and Barnabas stoutly and sternly refused worship (Acts 14:11-15).

(3) He did works which only God can perform. He forgave sin (Mark 2:5-7); He raised the dead (John 11:43); He raised Himself from the dead (John 2:19; 10:18); He created the world (Col. 1:16); He sustains the world (Col. 1:17; Heb. 1:2-3); His miracles attest His glory and His deity (John 2:11).

(4) Divine attributes prove that Jesus Christ is God. He is omnipotent (Matt. 28:18); omnipresent (Matt. 28:20); omniscient (John 21:17; 2:25; 16:30; Acts 1:24); eternal (John 1:1; Col. 1:17; John 8:58).

(5) As shown under section II, 3, of this lesson, names applied to Jehovah God in the Old Testament are applied to Christ in the New Testament.

(6) The association of the name of Christ with that of God and the Holy Spirit in a way that would exclude all other names, points to the conclusion that the three are co-equal. Matt. 28:19; II Cor. 13:14; John 10:30. When Christ spoke of God as His Father in a unique sense, the Jews understood Him to mean that He was making Himself equal with God (John 5:18). The

chief priests and scribes considered Christ's affirmation
of His deity as just grounds for putting Him to death
(Luke 22:70). There are innumerable cults, churches
and clergy who would lift their voices with the assassins of
that day and say, "Away with Him, let Him be crucified," on the same ground.

I Tim. 3:16
John 1:14
Phil. 2:5-7

c. Christ is the God-Man. While it is true that
Christ was human, He was God manifest in the flesh.
Christ did not lay aside His deity when He came to tent in
human flesh. Paul explains that He, Who was equal with
God, *took* (*taking* is not *subtraction* but *addition*) on
Him the form of a servant and was made in the likeness

II Cor. 5:18

of men. "God was in Christ" in reconciling the world unto Himself. To say that Christ is dead, forever dead, is
ample proof that the so-called "Jehovah's Witnesses" are
"false witnesses" in the light of the superabundant testimony of the New Testament—Acts 1:3; I Cor. 15.

Heb. 1:4, 6

d. Christ was never Michael the archangel. Christ is
so much better than the angels. Angels worship Christ.
The first chapter of Hebrews shows clearly that Christ

Heb. 1:6

is *better* than angels inasmuch as, in relationship, a son
excels a servant; in dignity, the One worshipped excels

Heb. 1:7-8

the worshippers; in position, Christ as Sovereign Lord

Heb. 1:9

excels the angels who are but subjects; in holiness, in
that Christ hated iniquity whereas there were angels that

II Pet. 2:4

sinned. Michael had to implore divine help from the

Jude 9

Lord when disputing with the devil over the body of
Moses, thus distinguishing him from the Lord and showing his inferiority.

When it is remembered that the word "angel" simply
denotes "messenger" then it should not occasion any confusion when the Bible refers to the messengers of the
seven churches in Rev. 2-3, as "angels." And likewise the
prophet Malachi, meaning "My messenger" uses the word
to refer to both John the Baptist and Christ (Mal. 3:1).
Zechariah uses the terms "Angel of Jehovah" and "Jehovah" synonymously (Zech. 1:12-13). Christ is the Angel
of Jehovah in the sense that He conveys God's message to
men and is thus *the* Messenger.

Examination on Lesson XVI

Marks

6 1. Give at least six important historical facts about the life of Charles T. Russell.

3 2. What vital contribution to the movement was made by J. F. Rutherford?

3 3. Who is the present president and what was his contribution?

15 4. Quote Isa. 43 :11; Acts 4:12; 1:8.

10 5. In calling themselves witnesses unto Jehovah God but not witnesses unto Christ, prove that they are out of joint with the teaching of the New Testament.

10 6. Prove that Jesus is Jehovah.

3 7. What passages do they misuse to prove that Jesus was created?

10 8. What answer would you give to their contention?

20 9. Give at least ten Scriptural reasons with references why you believe in the deity of Christ.

10 10. How would you disprove their contention that Christ was originally a created angel known as Michael?

10 11. Give at least ten references in the gospels which prove that Christ accepted worship. You may use your Bible.

100

LESSON XVII

"JEHOVAH'S WITNESSES" (Continued)

2. Eternal punishment.

They teach:

a. That hell, the grave, Sheol, Gehenna and Hades are all synonymous terms. In an anonymous book published by the Watch Tower and Tract Society, entitled *Let God Be True,* pp. 72-73, they say, "It is so plain that the Bible hell is the tomb, the grave, that even an honest little child can understand it, but not the religious theologians." On page 68 of the same book they say, "A fiery hell is a God-dishonouring religious doctrine." On page 80, the writer affirms: "It is clearly seen that hell or sheol or hades means the grave, the tomb, the condition where all, good and bad, go awaiting the day of resurrection."

b. A second chance. They teach that all who die without Christ will have another chance. They will have the gospel preached to them, and if they do not then wish to accept the invitation, they will be annihilated. On pp. 77-78 of *Let God Be True* they say, "Gehenna is a picture or symbol of complete annihilation or extermination, and not of eternal torment." And on page 80 it reads, "Gehenna is the condition of destruction where the Devil, his demons and all opposers of the Theocratic Government of Jehovah God will go and from which condition there is no recovery or resurrection."

Those refusing the second chance will be annihilated by the second death, which is extinction. God is too good, they say, to sustain an existence so useless and injurious to itself. They consider it absurd to suppose that God would perpetuate existence forever in torment.

We reply:

The Hebrew word for "grave" is *qeber* (pronounced

135

"kawbar"). It is used sixty-seven times in the Old Testament. It is used in the plural as well as the singular. As might be expected, its use in the Old Testament makes it clear that a grave is something which men may dig, buy, place their dead in, touch, sprinkle dust upon, etc. For example:

(1) Graves may be personal property, dug, located in a country (Gen. 50:5).

(2) There are many graves (Exod. 14:11).

(3) A grave may be touched (Num. 19:16, 18).

(4) People weep at a grave (II Sam. 3:32).

(5) The body of a dead man may be laid in a grave (I Kings 13:30).

(6) One grave may be located alongside another (II Sam. 19:37).

(7) Bodies may be buried in a grave (I Kings 14:13).

(8) Men may sprinkle dust on a grave (II Kings 23:6).

The Hebrew word *Sheol* appears 65 times in the Old Testament. Unfortunately, in our Authorized Version, this Hebrew word is translated "grave" 31 times, "hell" 31 times and "pit" three times. It would have saved much confusion if the word had been rendered simply *Sheol,* as in the A.R.V. The meaning of a word must be determined by its use in the context. That Sheol is not the grave can be proved as follows:

a. Although our Authorized Version speaks in Gen. 37:35 of Jacob going to the "grave" to meet his son, the Hebrew word *Sheol* in this verse cannot mean the grave because Jacob thought that Joseph was devoured by beasts and therefore would not be buried in a grave. Nobody goes *mourning* into a grave. Nobody can go to another in a grave.

b. In Deut. 32:22, the same word *Sheol* is wrongly translated "hell." Here we notice fire is associated with *Sheol* and that God's anger reaches to the "lowest part" of *Sheol.* There is no fire in a grave and there would be no point in saying that God's anger will extend to the lowest *Sheol* if Sheol meant the grave, for man's anger could go that far.

c. In II Sam. 22:6 it speaks of the sorrows of *Sheol.* But there are no sorrows in a grave.

d. In Job 11:8 the depth of Sheol is contrasted with the height of heaven. Obviously there would be no contrast if *Sheol* were the grave. See also Ps. 139:8 and Amos 9:2.

e. In Ps. 9:17 it speaks of great numbers of wicked being put in *Sheol.* You cannot get many wicked into one grave but there is room for nations in *Sheol.*

f. In Ps. 16:10, it speaks of the soul going to *Sheol.* It also speaks of that which can corrupt. The body is corruptible: the soul is incorruptible. This passage is prophetic and Messianic as proved by Peter's use of it in Acts in applying it to Christ.

This passage in Acts 2:31 also shows that *Sheol* and *Hades* are identical for the Hebrew word *Sheol* from Ps. 16:10 is in the Greek *Hades.* Combining the Old with the New Testament idea, we might speak of the underworld as "Sheol-Hades."

g. In Ps. 55:15 it shows that even when death has seized the wicked, their souls will go alive into *Sheol.* How obvious it is that *Sheol* is *not* the grave!

h. *Sheol* is associated with pain in Ps. 116:3 but there is no pain in a grave.

i. The house of the lascivious woman is the way to *Sheol.* If *Sheol* is just the grave, then a wicked woman is as well off as the virtuous woman. Moreover her guests "are in the depths of Sheol" (Prov. 7:27; 9:18). To teach that *Sheol* is the grave is to cast off all moral restraint, make sin a joke and become like those of whom it is said, "There is no fear of God before their eyes."

Rom. 3:18

j. Wicked address other wicked descending into *Sheol.* In Isa. 14:9, the same Hebrew word *Sheol,* translated "hell" in verse 11, is translated "grave." This is misleading from the standpoint of our Authorized Version for the English words are not synonymous.

k. *Sheol* is never full but a grave can soon be filled. Prov. 27:20; Isa. 5:14.

Luke 16:19-21
The Greek word *Hades* is used eleven times in the New Testament and is translated "hell" ten times and "grave" once. In *Hades* men are (1) self-conscious, (2) able to talk, (3) tormented, (4) separated and far off from those who are comforted, (5) able to remember, (6) in flames, (7) without mercy, not even a drop of water to cool the tongue. Christ gives a revelation of what lies beyond the pale of death for a righteous man in contrast to the wicked.

II Cor. 12:2
There seems to be a very close resemblance between physical and soulical sensibilities. Paul was not able to discern the difference. Even when we reflect on our dreams it is difficult to discern, sometimes, whether our experiences were physiological or just psychological. Furthermore we are in no position to say whether a disembodied spirit is destitute of such sensibilities as sight, pain, etc. Man made in the similitude of God, may like God be able to see, hear, feel and be self-conscious even when disembodied. At any rate, it is clearly spoken that after Dives was buried, that is, after his body was buried, he lifted up eyes which could see and discern and he had a passionate desire for water.

Matt. 10:28

Mark 9:43, 45, 47
l. The Greek word *Gehenna* is used eleven times in the New Testament and is translated "hell." Christ spoke of Gehenna as being a place of fire, fire that "never shall be quenched." In eight of the eleven times it is used, the fire is spoken of as being "everlasting." Very obviously, *Gehenna* cannot mean the grave.

Rom. 16:26

I Tim. 1:17

Heb. 9:14

Rev. 1:18

Matt. 19:29

John 6:54, 58

Matt. 25:46
m. The use of the word "eternal" to express the endless duration of God the Father, God the Son and God the Holy Spirit, the future happiness of the saints as well as the eternal misery of the lost, proves that the suffering of the wicked continues through eternity. The use of the word in Revelation proves that it means "endless duration," "ages of ages," "forever and ever." See Rev. 1:6; 4:9-10; 5:13; 7:12; 10:6; 11:15; 14:10-11; 19:3; 20:10. The suffering of the wicked is as endless as the existence of God.

Concerning annihilation *we reply:*

I Tim. 5:6

Luke 9:60

Eph. 2:1-3

John 5:24

Rom. 6:23

a. It does not say in Rev. 21:8 that the lake of fire *produces* the second death but it *is* the second death. Death in the Scripture nowhere means extinction of being, or non-existence. When used in the penal aspect it means wrong existence, wretched, debased, or devilish existence.

b. To perish does not mean annihilation. When the wine bottles of Matt. 9:17 perished, they ceased to function for the purpose for which they were made. When a soul perishes it cannot function for the purpose for which it was created, to glorify God (Col. 1:16).

Hosea 4:6

John 2:19

c. To destroy does not mean to annihilate. Hosea lamented concerning Israel, "My people are *destroyed* for lack of knowledge" but he did not mean that the people had been annihilated. When Jesus said, "*Destroy* this temple and in three days I will raise it up again," He did not mean *annihilate* this temple." Some hold that sin has such effect upon the soul as ultimately to destroy it. This cannot be, for the greater the sin, the sooner the sinner would be destroyed and the punishment would be disproportionate.

II Cor. 6:2

Heb. 9:27

Prov. 29:1

Matt. 25:41
Matt. 8:12
Matt. 13:42
Rev. 14:10-11
Matt. 25:46
Rom. 2:5
Rev. 21:8
II Thess. 1:9
Matt. 10:15

d. As for a second chance, the Bible does not teach any chance after death. It does teach that *now* is the accepted time and the day of salvation. It does say that after death comes the judgment. It does say that "he that being often reproved, hardeneth his neck, shall suddenly be destroyed and that *without remedy*." There are many passages to show that the state of the wicked at death is fixed and final: (1) Eternal fire, (2) Darkness, (3) Wailing and gnashing of teeth, (4) Torment, (5) Eternal punishment, (6) Wrath of God, (7) Second death, (8) Eternal destruction.

3. The kingdom.

They teach:

a. That Christ's kingdom was fully established in 1914. See *Basis for Belief in a New World*, published by the Watch Tower in 1953, page 49.

b. Christ's second coming is as invisible as the wind (John 14:19) (*Ibid.*).

c. Many happenings taken together would constitute the sign of His second presence as King.

d. That "in the last days of this old world and at the portals of a new world Jehovah's Witnesses preach the good news of the established kingdom and show how Jehovah's battle of Armageddon will cleanse the earth of wickedness and open the way to endless peace, happiness and life. This preaching work causes a separation of the people, some for the incoming new world and some against it (Matt. 25:31-46). Opposers persecute the witnesses declaring this good news and scoff and sneer at the warning being proclaimed" (Ibid., p. 51).

Isa. 2:2-4
Micah 4:1-5
Zech. 14:9-11
Rev. 11:15
Ps. 2
Dan. 2:44
Matt. 6:10

Acts 1:11
Matt. 24:30
Rev. 1:7

Matt. 24:29

24:15, 21, 30

24:6

Mark 16:15
Matt. 28:20
Rom. 1:16
Rom. 15:20
Acts 28:23
Gal. 1:7-9
I Cor. 15:1-4
Heb. 4:2

We reply:

a. That Christ's kingdom was *not* fully established in 1914. If it had been, wars would have ceased and the kingdom of this world would now have been the Kingdom of our Lord. When the King comes, His will will be done on earth as it is in heaven.

b. Christ's coming is visible.

c. In Matt. 24, the signs precede His coming and then *immediately after* the revelation of the Man of sin and the Great Tribulation, the Son of man *appears*. Christ admonished His disciples not to confuse signs with the sign.

d. "The gospel" of Matt. 24:14 was a gospel being preached by Christ and the apostles and the same gospel was to be preached unto the consummation of the age. The gospel of the kingdom is not a different gospel to that which Paul preached and which every true minister of the gospel preaches today.

Examination on Lesson XVII

Marks

5   1. What do "Jehovah's Witnesses" teach about hell?

5   2. What do they teach about a second chance?

15   3. What is the Hebrew word for "grave" and how is it used in the O.T.? Illustrate your answer from Scripture.

25   4. Concerning the Hebrew word *Sheol,* how often is it used in the O.T., how is it translated in our Authorized version and how can it be proved that Sheol is not the grave?

10   5. How can it be proved that the Hebrew place called *Sheol* is identical with the place called *Hades* in the Greek N.T.?

10   6. What does the N.T. teach about *Hades?* How often is the term used in the Greek? How is it translated?

3   7. What does Paul's experience recorded in II Cor. 12:1-3 indicate with respect to the close relationship between physiological and psychological experience?

7   8. How is the Greek word *Gehenna* used? Prove that *Gehenna* cannot mean the grave. Distinguish between *Hades* and *Gehenna.*

10   9. How does the use of the word "eternal" in the N.T. point to the conclusion that the punishment of the wicked is everlasting?

10   10. Prove that the Russelite teaching on annihilation is without scriptural foundation.

10   11. Prove that their doctrine of a second chance is likewise contrary to the teaching of the Scripture.

12   12. What do they teach about the Kingdom?

10   13. Give Scripture references to prove that Christ's Kingdom was not fully established in 1914.

10   14. Prove that Christ's coming will be visible.

10   15. Prove that the signs *precede* His coming.

16   16. Prove that Matt. 24:14 refers to the one gospel of Christ.

$$\frac{168 \times 100}{168} = 100$$

LESSON XVIII

SEVENTH DAY ADVENTISTS

I. *History.*

William Miller of Low Hampton, New York, dogmatically and widely proclaimed that Christ would return in 1844. He based his prediction on a year-day interpretation of Daniel 8:14. Mrs. Ellen G. White, in her book *The Great Controversy Between Christ and Satan,* on page 375, says:

> . . . the beginning of the seventy weeks is fixed beyond question at B.C. 457, and their expiration in A.D. 34. From this data there is no difficulty in finding the termination of the 2300 days. The seventy weeks—490 days—having been cut off from the 2300, there were 1810 days remaining. After the end of 490 days, the 1810 days were still to be fulfilled. From A.D. 34, 1810 years extend to 1844. Consequently the 2300 days of Daniel 8:14 terminated in 1844. At the expiration of this great prophetic period upon the testimony of the angel of God, "The sanctuary shall be cleansed." Thus the time of the cleansing of the sanctuary—which was almost universally believed to take place at the second advent—was definitely pointed out.

Much to his embarrassment, Christ did not return in 1844. In order to cover Mr. Miller's error, Mrs. Ellen G. White, one of his diligent devotees, conceived the idea that Christ did return in 1844 and entered upon a second phase of His redemptive work, a work of "investigative judgment." Thus she writes on page 481:

> Thus those who followed in the light of the prophetic word saw that, instead of coming to the earth at the termination of the 2300 days in 1844, Christ then entered the most holy place of the holy sanctuary, to perform the closing work of atonement, preparatory to His coming.

143

According to Mrs. White, there were three phases to Christ's work of redemption. The first was His work on the cross which, she said, compared to the work of the Jewish priests at the brazen altar. The second was the work He began in 1844 when He went into the sanctuary to carry on a work of investigative judgment examining the records of men, especially with reference to their keeping the law and particularly the fourth commandment. The third phase will begin on the Day of Atonement when Christ will go into the most holy place, lay our sins upon the scapegoat Satan, who will carry them off to oblivion. In this connection she says, on page 481:

> It was seen, also, that while the sin offering pointed to Christ as a sacrifice, and the high priest represented Christ as a mediator, the scapegoat typified Satan, the author of sin, upon whom the sins of the truly penitent will finally be placed. . . . The scapegoat was sent away into a land not inhabited, never to come again into the congregation of Israel. So will Satan be forever banished from the presence of God and His people, and he will be blotted from existence in the final destruction of sin and sinners.

In one of Mrs. White's visions, she is supposed to have seen Christ carrying on this work of investigative judgment and pointing to the fourth commandment, the keeping of the Sabbath. The birth of the cult was thus brought to a culmination, and so she writes on page 497:

> The conviction was urged upon them, that they had ignorantly transgressed this precept by disregarding the Creator's rest day. . . . They had been honestly seeking to know and to do God's will; now, as they saw themselves transgressors of His law, sorrow filled their hearts, and they manifested their loyalty to God by keeping His Sabbath holy.

Thus they gave themselves the name, "Seventh Day Adventists." But, strange to say, this cult has sought assiduously and quite successfully to obscure its identity. Their "Voice of Prophecy" broadcasts, heard each *Sun-*

day over stations on every continent have allured thousands of unwary souls into their net. I have met people who were enrolled in their free Bible-correspondence courses who were amazed when told that they were enrolled in a course on Seventh Day Adventism. Satan's pills are sugar-coated. Through a very subtle but Satanic subterfuge they have gone to every mission field and practiced their proselyting on Christian converts after missionaries may have laboured for years to gain a foothold. To my knowledge, they resort to this method exclusively, doing no pioneer work among raw pagans but directing their energies solely toward the turning aside of those set free, to legalism. Being a very lucrative organization, they have been able to buy off many followers through man's innate love for earthly gain and gold.

II. *Their doctrines.*

1. Concerning the Sabbath *they teach:*

a. That the Pope, the Antichrist, changed the Sabbath from Saturday to Sunday and that all who keep Sunday bear the mark of the Beast and will go to hell for violating God's Sabbath day (See *The Great Controversy,* pp. 510-513).

b. Some claim that Constantine, the Roman Emperor changed the day.

c. They claim that Saturday, the seventh day, was instituted by God Himself from the very dawn of creation. That when God rested on the Sabbath, He set an example for all generations to follow and called upon all men to "Remember the Sabbath day to keep it holy." The institution of the Sabbath, they maintain, was never abrogated (Ibid. p. 510).

We reply:

a. There have been many Popes, but normally, never more than one at a time. In the time of the apostle John there were many antichrists (I John 2:18). In the same passage John spoke of Antichrist who would

Dan. 7:25-27

II Thess. 2:8

Rev. 13

Rev. 19:10-21

II Thess. 2:3

come "in the last time." *The* Antichrist will rule the world just prior to Christ's Coming, at which time He will be destroyed, that is, cast into the lake of fire. Since *the* Antichrist has not *yet* been revealed, it is obvious that he cannot be blamed for changing the Sabbath. Then it follows that those who observe Sunday can not be regarded as wearing the mark of the Beast. The specifications set down in Rev. 13:16-18 for the mark of the beast have nothing whatever to do with Sunday observance.

b. It cannot be proved on historical ground that Constantine *changed* the day. When he, the Roman Emperor, was converted to Christianity, he simply endorsed a custom already in practice and made Sunday a legal holiday for all people in the Empire.

Rom. 14:5-6

c. We do not believe that one's salvation is determined by the keeping of Saturday or Sunday. "One man esteemeth one day above another: another esteemeth every day alike. Let every man be fully persuaded in his own mind. He that regardeth the day, regardeth it unto the Lord; and he that regardeth not the day, to the Lord he doth not regard it." The vital issues of the Christian life lie much deeper than the observance of "days and months and times and years."

What is God teaching us in the Old Testament Sabbath that is preparatory to the enactment of redemption? The cross is the focal point of history. Is it merely physical rest that God had in mind? That has its value but God has been seeking all down through the corridors of time to bring a restless world to rest in Him alone for both salvation and service.

Matt.   11:28-30

Rom. 4:4-5

Isa. 40:28

Before the first creation was marred by sin, God rested. God did not rest because He was weary. God is Spirit. God does not get tired. He is omnipotent. But when sin wrenched man from fellowship with God, God began to work for man's redemption and in the fulness of time He brought forth His only Son to accomplish redemption for us. When on the cross, He shouted in triumph, "It is finished!" He made a way of access into the presence of God for us. Christ ascended to the right

Heb. 1:3

Heb. 9:12

hand of the Father and *sat down*. Having accomplished eternal redemption for us, He invites a weary world, "Come unto me all ye that labor and are heavy-laden and I will give you rest." Those who would enter into *His* rest *must* cease from their own works.

Heb. 4:10
Rom. 4:4-5
Exod. 20:8-11
Exod. 16:27-29
Exod. 35:2-3
Num. 15:32-36
Exod. 31:13-18

Gal. 3:10

Why did God insist on pain of death that positively *no* work was to be done on the Sabbath? To gather manna on the Sabbath, to pick up sticks on the Sabbath, to even leave the house on the Sabbath exposed the law-breaker to the penalty of death. It sounds very solemn and severe and indeed it is for "Cursed is every one that continueth not in *all* things which are written in *the* law to *do* them (not just try to do them)." But when one remembers that here God is dealing with a principle regarding salvation that this human race is so slow to learn, it is not at all severe. It simply reveals the perfect harmony of God's revelation of redemption and

Rom. 11:6
Eph. 2:8-9

salvation. Not until man stops all his working to save himself and trusts only in Christ's finished work, can he be saved. To get a man to see that salvation is by grace alone, is the biggest barrier to successful soul-winning. To get a man to see that *all* his righteousnesses

Isa. 64:6

are as filthy rags and that he must come as expressed in the spirit of that immortal hymn:

> Nothing in my hand I bring
> Simply to Thy cross I cling;
> Naked, come to Thee for dress,
> Helpless look to Thee for grace;
> Foul, I to the fountain fly,
> Help me, Saviour, or I die,

is the principle that distinguishes Christianity from every other religious system of proffered salvation.

Matt. 11:28
Matt. 11:29
Col. 1:29
Eph. 3:20
John 6:63
John 15:6

This rest into which the believer enters in salvation, is also the rest in which he is called to live and serve. It is the life in which we substitute His mighty working for our fruitless efforts. "The flesh profiteth nothing." Dr. A. B. Simpson expressed it this way in his wonderful hymn, "Once it was the Blessing, now it is the Lord,":

> Once it was my working, His it hence shall be;
> Once I tried to use Him; now He uses me.

Josh. 1:15
Josh. 24:12-13

Josh. 24

Heb. 11:30

Zech. 4:6

Heb. 4:10

Matt. 28:1
Gal. 6:15
II Cor. 5:17
Lev. 23:7, 11,
15, 16, 21,
24, 28, 32,
35, 39, 40;
25:10
Rom. 8:2
Gal. 5:18, 25

It was typified in the Canaan rest when God's redeemed people crossed their Jordan to the conquest of
seven nations much greater and mightier than they.
God *gave* them that land. The *Lord* fought for Israel.
By *faith* the walls of Jericho fell down. The Lord delivered their enemies into their hands. And it is no
secret what *God* can do. The principle obtains throughout all time that it is *not* by might, nor by power, but
by my Spirit saith the Lord. The Christian, who enters
into that *rest,* has been persuaded that it is much better
to cease from his own works and let God work through
him.

The resurrection of Christ from the dead on the first
day of the week opened the way to the establishment of
a new creation based on an accomplished redemption.
The first day Sabbath was foreshadowed in the Old
Testament. It is brought into full realization in the
New Testament and in the life of each one who has
been made a new creation in Christ Jesus. Walking in
the Spirit, the believer walks in liberty, free from the
law of sin and death.

2. Concerning salvation, *they teach:*

a. The keeping of the law is necessary as evidence
of salvation. Believers who fail in observing Saturday
are lost. When Christ returns, only 144,000 will be
saved and these will be Adventists who do not have
the mark of the Beast upon them. Faith in Christ can
only obtain remission for sins that are past but the
law of God is the standard by which the character and
the lives of men will be tested in the judgment (See
The Great Controversy Between Christ and Satan,
pp. 533-534).

b. As pointed out in the History of the Movement,
they teach that there are three phases to Christ's work
of redemption. The cross was only the first stage of
redemption. The second stage began in 1844 when Christ
entered the sanctuary to begin His work of "investigative
judgment." The third stage is when our sins are laid
upon the scapegoat Satan on the Day of Atonement.

We reply:

Eph. 2:8-9
Rom. 4:4-5

Acts 16:31

Gal. 3:10

Acts 15:5

Acts 15:24

I Pet. 2:24

Heb. 8:1-2

a. Salvation is *not* by works. Salvation is not a co-operative matter in which we mix our human efforts with the holy efficacy of His atoning blood. Jesus Himself is the Saviour, the only Saviour. Faith in *Him* implies our looking away from ourselves to *Him* alone. To attempt attaining to salvation through the keeping of the law is vain "For it is written, 'Cursed is every man that continueth not in *all things* which are written in the book of the law (the entire Pentateuch) to *do* them'" (not merely *trying* to do them but complete obedience).

In Acts 15 we read that "There rose up certain of the sect of the Pharisees which believed, saying 'That it was needful to circumcise them and to command them to keep the law of Moses.'" But the verdict reached by the apostles and elders was, "We have heard that certain which went out from us have troubled you with words, *subverting your souls,* saying, 'Ye must be circumcised and keep the law': 'to whom *we gave no such commandment.*'" Any one claiming to be a member of the 144,000 of Rev. 7, should also be prepared to tell you to what tribe of Israel he belongs.

b. According to John 1:29, Christ is the Lamb of God Who beareth away the sin of the world. Christ bore our sin in His own body on the tree. The writer of Hebrews makes it very plain that Christ has already obtained eternal redemption for us (9:12) and that by *one* offering He hath made full atonement for our sin. Not in 1844 did Christ enter the sanctuary but, having accomplished full redemption for us at the cross, He ascended to the right hand of the Majesty in the heaven and began His ministry as our High-Priest and Intercessor in the heavenly sanctuary.

3. Concerning immortality, *they teach:*

Conditional immortality. By this they mean that only some souls will be immortal, those who are in possession of eternal life. Carlyle B. Haynes, in his book, *Seventh*

Day Adventists—Their Work and Teachings, p. 19,
says, "Man is mortal. And his only hope of living for ever
is dependent, therefore and conditional upon union with
God through Christ our Saviour, who has promised
eternal life to all who believe in Him." The rest, they
say, will be annihilated and will cease to exist. Their
reasoning is that since eternal life means eternal existence,
then eternal death means eternal non-existence. They
hold that the wicked, including Satan, the author of
sin, will be destroyed by the fires of the last days and
be finally reduced to a state of non-existence, becoming
as though they had not been (p. 27).

We reply:

Eternal life means more than eternal existence. A
chair has existence but not life. In I John 5:12 we
learn that he that hath the Son, hath life and this
eternal life is in God's Son. Life in the Bible refers
to life in right relationship to God and for this purpose
Christ came that we might have life. It would be foolish
to say that a sinner "dead in trespasses and sins" was
"non-existent." How ludicrous it would be to interpret
Christ's admonition to let the dead bury their dead as
meaning, "Let the non-existent bury the non-existent."
Death, they say, is a complete cessation of life but
Scripture indicates that physical death simply suspends
the union between the body and the soul till the resurrection. Thus Paul speaks of physical death as being
"absent from the body but present with the Lord." After
1000 years of torment in the lake of fire, the beast and
the false prophet are still existent (Cp. Rev. 19:20
with Rev. 20:10). Furthermore, how can a non-existent
person be tormented? Yet the Bible declares that the
devil will be tormented forever (Rev. 20:10).

4. Concerning soul-sleeping, *they teach:*

"Human consciousness depends on the union of the
breath of life with the body. When these two are separated
at death, unconsciousness is bound to follow. Man at
death lapses into unconsciousness. The Bible calls this

sleep. That state of unconsciousness and the duration of that sleep continue until the time of man's awakening and resurrection from the dead" (*Seventh-Day Adventists, Their Work and Teachings,* by Carlyle B. Haynes, p. 21).

We reply:

John 4:24
Heb. 1:14
Heb. 12:23

Spirit is not dependent for activity and consciousness on its possession of a body. If that were true, then God, angels and the disembodied "spirits of just men" would not be conscious, nor active. Such passages as Ps. 6:5; 146:4; Eccl. 9:10; Dan. 12:2; Matt. 9:24; John 11:11; I Cor. 15:51; I Thess. 4:14 must not be interpreted in the face of clear Scripture testimony to the contrary. These passages are to be regarded as the language of appearance, and as literally applicable to the body. The rich man of Luke 16:19-31 must have been having a dreadful nightmare if he was *merely* asleep. If the souls of Rev. 6:9-10, after being slain, were able to cry with a loud voice, "How long O Lord, holy and true, dost Thou not judge and avenge our blood on them that dwell on the earth?" then it is very evident that soul-sleepers do not sleep very soundly. Paul, who was "in death oft" confessed to an experience, likely his own, when he was "caught up to the third

II Cor. 12:2-4

heaven and *heard unspeakable words,* which it is not lawful to utter." He himself did not know whether he was "in the body" or "out of the body." It is presumptuous to say that a person who leaves the body to be present

II Cor. 5:8
Ps. 16:11

with the Lord, is unconscious for "In His presence there is fulness of joy."

A conference of leaders of the Seventh-Day Adventists with Donald Grey Barnhouse and Walter R. Martin of *Eternity* magazine and with George Cannon of Nyack Missionary College, indicates that a change may be taking place within the movement. Submitting forty questions to the Adventist leaders, Mr. Martin received a lengthy written reply. After poring over the questions and answers in days of detailed discussion, he came to the following conclusions:

(1) Present day Adventists do not regard the writings of Mrs. Ellen G. White to be on parity with the Scriptures.

(2) Sabbath-keeping is in no way a means of salvation.

(3) Jesus was in no way a created being.

(4) They believe in the finished work of Christ. They hold that the bearing of our sin into oblivion by the scapegoat to be a kind of "legal" transaction but not a vicarious bearing of sin on the Cross.

(5) They still hold to the doctrine of the "investigative judgment."

(6) They do hold that the keeping of Saturday is necessary for any Christian seeking to walk in obedience to God's commandments.

(7) They adhere to the belief in conditional immortality (i.e., soul-sleeping and the annihilation of the lost).

This lesson on the present Seventh-Day Adventists, is based on the previous publications, eminently those of Mrs. Ellen G. White, whom they still revere as one who had special counsels from God for their movement. If they have been going through a process of conversion over the past few years let us hope for their full recovery.

Examination on Lesson XVIII

Marks

10 1. How did Mr. Miller and Mrs. White reach the conclusion that something very significant was going to happen in 1844?

10 2. Explain the three phases of Christ's atoning work according to Mrs. White.

5 3. Make clear how they came to be called Seventh-Day Adventists.

6 4. What do they teach about the Sabbath?

24 5. How do you reply to each one of the three tenets regarding Sabbath?

8 6. What do they teach about salvation?

12 7. What is your reply?

6 8. What do they teach about immortality?

12 9. What is your reply?

10 10. What do they teach about soul-sleeping?

22 11. How do you answer this?

$125 \times \dfrac{100}{125} = 100$

LESSON XIX

CHRISTIAN SCIENCE

I. *History.*

While outwardly Christian Science might be regarded as the religion of the refined, inwardly it is the religion of the refusal and rejection of every cardinal doctrine of the Christian faith. It is neither Christian nor Science. Mrs. Mary Baker Eddy is the foundress of the movement. Her book, *Christian Science with Key to the Scriptures,* is regarded by her followers as the key to the understanding of the Scriptures. She claims that her work was inspired. It was published in 1875.

She obtained the radical and distinctive features of her system, the cure of disease by the power of mind, from a man named Dr. P. P. Quimby, who had written ten volumes elaborating a system of mental healing without the aid of medicine.

In her early years, Mary Baker Eddy was subject to fits of hysteria which often sent her to the floor writhing and screaming in apparent agony. At other times, she became rigid and motionless. Her father remarked, "The Bible says that Mary Magdalene had seven devils, but our Mary has got ten." This condition followed her into womanhood. She was married to a bricklayer, named "George Washington Glover" in 1843. She referred to him as "Colonel." In six months he died. In 1853 she married Daniel Patterson, an itinerant dentist. They were divorced. In 1877 she married Asa Gilbert, whom she referred to as "Dr. Eddy" though he was but a sewing-machine agent. She gave distinguished degrees and titles to all three of her husbands.

The Mother Church, the *First Church of Christ, Scientist,* is at Boston. It has gained much popularity among the refined and educated peoples of America and Canada. Its metaphysical philosophy of life meets with acceptance among peoples who have known little about the rugged realities of hardship and suffering.

The Christian Science Journal, now in its seventy-fourth year of continuous publication, claims Christian Science to be the fulfillment of Christ's return. In the issue for December, 1948, it reads, "Christian Science is the Second Coming of Christ, the appearing of man as the Son of God which comes to human consciousness to destroy embodied evil."

II. *Heresies.*

1. Concerning God, *they teach:*

a. In her book *Science and Health with Key to the Scriptures,* p. 465, Mrs. Eddy says, "God is incorporeal, divine, supreme, infinite mind, Spirit, Soul, Principle, Life, Truth, Love." God is not a person, but merely a principle.

b. God is not a trinity. "The theory of three persons in one God, suggests polytheism rather than the one ever present 'I AM'" (*Ibid.,* p. 256).

We reply:

a. If we deny the personality of God, we must also deny our own personality, for man was made in "the likeness and image of God." Personal names such as Father, Shepherd, Captain, Healer, Lord, Husband, Husbandman, Deliverer, King, etc. show that God is a person. Personal pronouns, referring to God, abound in the scriptures. Personal acts, such as forgiving sin, showing mercy, revealing, speaking, willing, protecting, providing, promising, confirming covenants, prove He is a person.

b. God is one in substance but there are three distinct persons subsisting eternally as Father, Son and Holy Spirit. The Hebrew word for God, *Elohim,* points to there being at least three persons in the Godhead (The Hebrew uses Singular, Dual and Plural numbers for its nouns: the word, *Elohim,* is plural). The use of a singular verb in Gen. 1:1, however, only points to the conclusion that God is one God, though not one person.

Matt. 6:26
Ps. 23:1
II Chron. 13:12
I Tim. 1:17
Exod. 15:26
Isa. 54:5
John 15:1

Gen. 1:26

Micah 7:18
Phil. 3:15
Matt. 6:24-33
Ps. 51:1
Ps. 91:1
II Cor. 1:20
Heb. 6:17-18

II Cor. 3:18
R.V.
Luke 1:35

Matt. 28:19
II Pet. 1:21
II Sam. 23:2
II Tim. 3:16

The word *Elohim* denotes a composite unity. The deity of Christ has been established in the lesson on "Jehovah's Witnesses." The deity of the Holy Spirit can likewise be established on the ground of the use of divine names, divine attributes, divine works, divine association and by the fact that works assigned to God in the Old Testament are accredited to the Holy Spirit in the New.

2. Concerning Jesus Christ and the denial of matter, *they teach:*

"Christ Jesus illustrated, by his entire life, the coincidence of the divine with the human. He appeared as a human being, but his knowledge of divine facts, that which constituted his Christ self-hood, existed entirely apart from the sense of a material body, even while he went about doing the ordinary things of life. He was able to heal the sick, raise the dead, and save the sinner, and in all of this he did not associate himself with the belief in matter. It was his absolute acknowledgment of the perfection of being that brought forth the evidence of healing and physical harmony" (Taken from a lecture given by a Christian Science practitioner in the Denver City Auditorium and submitted for publication to the Denver Colorado *Post,* March 26, 1948, p. 34).

We reply:

I John 1:1-2
I John 4:1-3

All of Jesus' miracles could be corroborated by the senses. He was heard, seen, handled. He touched the leper, walked, worked, ate, drank, slept and talked. Only a diseased mind or a devil-deceived one, could concoct such conglomerate nonsense as contained in the above paragraph setting forth the Christian Science concept of Christ.

3. Concerning the Holy Spirit, *they teach:*

That the promised Comforter was Divine Science. In Christian Science we have, they claim, the final and complete revelation of God and His Christ (Taken from a booklet of thirty-two pages published by the Christian Science Publishing Society in 1939, *A Prophet with Honor,* p. 26).

We reply:

This is a very blasphemous assumption. The promised Comforter came at Pentecost and through His blessed ministrations, men have been convicted of sin (the reality of which they deny), converted to Christ and conducted into paths of holiness and victory.

4. Concerning sin, *they teach:*

a. "Sin, sickness and death are to be classified as effects of error" (*Science and Health,* page 473).

b. "Man is incapable of sin, sickness and death" (*Ibid.,* p. 475).

We reply:

Isa. 53:6
Rom. 3:23
Acts 17:30
Rom. 5:12
John 3:16
Rom. 3:19

a. The universality of sin is proved by (1) the plain statements in the Word of God, (2) the universal need of repentance, (3) the universality of death, (4) the universal provision made for man's need, (5) universal guilt.

I John 5:17
Rom. 14:23
Jas. 4:17
Prov. 21:4
Prov. 24:9
I John 3:4
Rom. 1:18,
    24-30
Jer. 17:9

b. Man is capable of sin because: (1) All unrighteousness is sin, (2) whatsoever is not of faith is sin, (3) to him that knoweth to do good and doeth it not, to him it is sin, (4) an high look, a proud heart and the plowing of the wicked is sin, etc.

5. Concerning the Bible, it should be pointed out:

That although Mrs. Mary Baker Eddy has published a book that purports to give us the key to the scriptures, the key only opens the door to absolute absurdity. For example, she says Adam's name means "obstruction." How did she arrive at that conclusion? Well, says Mrs. Eddy, that is easy, "Adam is made up of two words, "a" and "dam" and a dam is an obstruction, so that is what "Adam" means. Yes, it is time to laugh. But when you consider that thousands of fine folk really believe this, we know that somebody needs to weep over their blindness and lostness. May it grip us.

Furthermore, let it be pointed out as Dr. Wilbur M. Smith has said in his book, *The Bible and the World Today,* with reference to Mrs. Eddy's book on Science and Health, "In its pages it expounds not the Scriptures, but only the first four chapters of Genesis, the Twenty-Third Psalm, and three chapters, 10, 12 and 21 from Revelation, as though these eight chapters were the principle part of the Word of God, rather than only a fragment. Notice that there are no chapters from the gospels, and none from the Epistles. The larger part of the Bible is ignored." How can her book be considered as a *key* to the *scriptures* when it ignores eleven hundred and eighty-one chapters of the Bible and gives such nonsensical interpretations of eight chapters?

Examination on Lesson XIX

Marks	
2	1. Who is the foundress of this movement and in what book does she set forth the beliefs of Christian Science?
2	2. From whom and how did she receive the distinctive features of her system?
6	3. What was characteristic of her early life and married life?
5	4. What is the name of the parent church? How do you account for its popularity among refined peoples?
4	5. How are Christian Science and the Second Coming of Christ related according to the Christian Science Journal?
6	6. What does Christian Science teach about God?
15	7. Give a full reply to each of these false tenets, using at least three Scripture references for each of the two points discussed in the lesson.
6	8. What do they teach about Jesus Christ and matter?
10	9. What is your reply and how serious is their claim in the light of Scripture?
2	10. What do they teach about the Holy Spirit?
10	11. Discuss why you believe this to be such a blasphemous doctrine.
6	12. What do they teach about sin?
15	13. Show five ways in which the universality of sin is proved. Give Scripture references for each.
6	14. Prove in four ways that man is capable of sin—using Scripture references.
5	15. Make clear the absurdity of their claim to giving us the key to the understanding of the Scriptures.
100	

LESSON XX

MORMONISM

I. *History.*

This movement had its beginning in America in the year 1827. It was organized by Joseph Smith and his associates at Fayette, Seneca County, New York, April 6, 1830. According to the story told by the founder of this religion, a man by the name of Moroni, who lived about 42 A.D., received a sacred record and was told to bring it forth in the latter days. When Joseph Smith was fourteen years of age, a heavenly messenger appeared to him, giving his name as Moroni. This messenger revealed the existence of a record engraved upon golden plates hidden in a hill between Palmyra and Manchester, New York. Four years later, on Sept. 22, 1827, the plates were delivered into Joseph's hands and with them instruments called "interpreters" (Urim and Thummim), by which he translated the cryptic characters found upon the plates and gave to the world *The Book of Mormon.* The ancient record was translated and published in 1830 (Taken from the *Encyclopaedia Britannica,* 1939 edition, Vol. XV, p. 800).

Joseph Smith was born December 23, 1805. His father sold blessings and his mother was a fortune-teller. Joseph was a man of great superstitions, strange dreams and visions, a man of great immorality and this he dignified by making of immorality a religion of which polygamy was one of the first principles. He had forty-nine wives. He died in 1844 at Carthage, Illinois, where he had been imprisoned by enraged farmers whose daughters he had taken in polygamy. The farmers mobbed the jail and murdered Smith (*Ibid.,* p. 809).

Brigham Young, successor of Joseph Smith and later prophet of Mormonism, was born in 1801 and died in 1877. In 1837 he was elected one of the twelve apostles.

161

When the apostle Joseph Smith was assassinated in 1844, Young was chosen president of the church to succeed him; and when he and his followers were expelled from Illinois, he led the way across the plains to the Great Salt Lake, where he founded Salt Lake City in 1847. He had seventeen wives and forty-seven children. In the capitol building of Salt Lake City, one may see a large frame on which are displayed the pictures of the wives of Brigham Young.

After the long, arduous journey across the plains to Utah, there developed a rift in the Mormon church. The "Josephites" were inclined to disown that they were Mormons because they averred that Joseph Smith did not teach or practice polygamy. The breach continued to widen as other issues were added. A controversy arose over the right of Brigham Young to be the successor to Joseph Smith: an issue developed over the inspiration of the book, *Pearl of Great Price,* "Josephites" claiming that it was not inspired: the question of whether the long hazardous trek to the West had been justified, was raised. The Utah Mormons or "Brighamites" with headquarters at Salt Lake City, came to regard the "Josephites" as apostates from the fold. The same attitude was held by the opposing faction which established headquarters at Independence, Missouri, and who call themselves "The Reorganized Church of the Latter-Day Saints."

However, the two factions have enough in common to warrant their being treated as one cult. Both say that Joseph Smith was the greatest prophet next to Jesus Christ. Each regards the *Book of Mormon* to be inspired and thus warrant their designation "Mormons" ("Mormon" means "both" implying belief in the Bible *and* the *Book of Mormon).* Both regard themselves as "Latter-Day Saints." Both factions have taught and practiced polygamy when occasion permitted and have listed twenty-two doctrines on which they agree.

According to the interpretation of the Mormon church, Ezek. 37:19-20 prophesied the union of the Bible, the stick of Judah, with the Book of Mormon, the stick of Joseph. The passage in the R. V. reads: "Say unto them, Thus saith the Lord Jehovah: Behold, I will take the stick of Joseph, which is in the hand of Ephraim, and the tribes of Israel his companions; and I will put them with it, even with the stick of Judah and make them one stick, and they shall be one in my hand. And the sticks whereon thou writest shall be in thine hand before their eyes." Notice if you will, that there is not a single word here about the Bible for the passage is not talking about the Bible but about the tribes of Israel.

Our reaction to these historical claims.

The claim of Joseph Smith to having been enabled to read Reformed Egyptian by the aid of Urim and Thummin from golden plates delivered to him by Moroni, is a very questionable one. Only the most credulous would believe that an uneducated boy would be able to read a language unknown to linguistic scholars today, written two thousand years ago. To think that these golden plates were kept in seclusion on this earth for approximately 1800 years and then whisked away so that there is no trace of a single one of these plates anywhere since they were reputedly read and translated by Joseph Smith, is more likely the dream of a moron. Moreover, it has been pointed out by Dr. Wilbur M. Smith that "in the first 428 pages of the text of the Book of Mormon, there are 298 direct quotations from the King James Version (made in A. D. 1611), in addition to entire chapters lifted out of that version of the Bible and placed in the Book of Mormon, without any hint that the passages are taken from the Bible. Is it not strange that Joseph Smith, in translating a book in Reformed Egyptian, inscribed two thousand years ago, should be led to translate passages word for word as the translators of the King James Version translated the Greek and Hebrew previous to 1611? This is direct plagiarism and deception." (*The Bible and the World Today,* p. 26).

"The Book of Mormon claims that there were three migrations to America: the first by Jared (Gen. 5:15; Luke 3:37), occurring soon after the dispersion of Babel; the second in 600 B.C., headed by Lehi, an Israelite of the tribe of Manasseh, whose name does not appear in the Bible; and the third, by a number of Israelites about eleven years later. Moreover the book says that Christ Himself came to America in A.D. 34 and 35, to repeat His Sermon on the Mount and to appoint twelve American Apostles . . . There is not one shred of historical evidence to support one of these statements regarding these three migrations and Christ's coming to America. And yet, out of this developed one of the outstanding religious movements of our country, born of a monstrous hoax, nothing more, garbed in the sanctities of Biblical terminology." (*Ibid.*, pp. 24-25).

The headquarters of the movement are in Salt Lake City, Utah, U.S.A. Mormon young men are expected to give two years of their time to "missionary work" and travel two-by-two propagating the doctrines of Mormonism. They operate in foreign fields, notably in the Philippine Islands, and have a large headquarters in Manila. There are over 70,000 members of the Mormon Church in Southern California and the largest Mormon temple in the world (not excluding the one in Salt Lake City) is located at Westwood, one of the swank suburbs of Los Angeles.

II. *Heresies.*

1. Concerning the scriptures, *they teach:*

a. "We believe the Bible to be the Word of God, so far as it is correctly translated; we also believe the Book of Mormon to be the Word of God." (Article 8 of the Mormon Catechism).

b. That the following books are also equal to the Bible in their inspiration: *Doctrines and Covenants, Pearl of Great Price, Journal of Discourses, The Seer, Articles of Faith, Key to Science and Theology, A Compendium.*

We reply:

"All Scripture is given by inspiration of God and is profitable for doctrine, for reproof, for correction, for instruction in righteousness" (II Tim. 3:16). To teach polygamy as "instruction in righteousness" contradicts the scriptures and so is unprofitable for doctrine, needs reproof and correction and therefore demonstrates that such writings are not divinely inspired. While cases of polygamy are recorded in the Bible, they are not approved. Any man having more than one wife, had his problems multiplied.

In II Pet. 1:21 we read concerning the inspiration of the scriptures that *holy men* of God were the instruments for the communication of God's Word to men. Joseph Smith definitely was not a holy man. We refuse to believe that his writings are on parity with the Scriptures.

God's final message was given through His Son for these last days and His message was communicated to us through His own chosen apostles by the Holy Spirit Who led them into *all the truth*. Men are forbidden to add to these writings.

Heb. 1:1-2
John 16:13
Rev. 22:18

2. Concerning God, *they teach:*

a. "To a Mormon, God is Adam. When our Father Adam came into the garden of Eden, he came into it with a celestial body and brought Eve, one of his wives with him . . . He is our Father and our God, and the only God with whom we have to do" (Brigham Young's *Journal of Discourses* Vol. VI, p. 50).

b. "It is clear that the Father is a personal being possessing a definite form, with bodily parts . . . We know that both the Father and the Son are in form and stature perfect men; each of them possess a tangible body, infinitely pure and perfect and attended by transcendant glory, nevertheless a body of flesh and bone" (Taken from James Talmage's book, *Articles of Faith,* pp. 41-42).

We reply:

a. John 4:24—"God is Spirit."
b. Luke 24:39—"A spirit hath not flesh and bones."

c. Col. 1:15—"The invisible God."

d. Jer. 23:24—"Can any hide himself in secret places that I shall not see him? saith the Lord. Do not I fill the heaven and earth? saith the Lord."

e. John 1:18—"No man hath seen God at any time; the only begotten Son, which is in the bosom of the Father, he hath declared him."

It is true that God has a form. Christ, before His incarnation in human flesh, is said to have been in "the form of God." But the Greek word for "form," *morphe,* simply denotes the sum total of all those qualities which make something to be the precise thing that it is. Jesus Christ was in possession of all the qualities that belong to God as God. Jesus Christ did not have a physical form of flesh and blood prior to His manifestation in the flesh when He *took a human nature.* Bodily parts are not essential elements of personality. The Holy Spirit is a person and yet He dwells in the heart of the believer. Satan entered into Judas, which is quite possible when one realizes that the devil and his angels are spirit beings.

3. Concerning man, *they teach:*

a. "One of the most beautiful truths that has been revealed to men through the restoration of the gospel in this dispensation, and one which sheds much light on so many matters, is the knowledge that all men lived with God and his Son, Jesus Christ, in the spirit world before they came here upon earth" (*A Marvellous Work and a Wonder,* by Le Grand Richards, p. 238).

b. "Man was also in the beginning with God, intelligence or the light of truth, was not created or made, neither indeed can be" (Joseph Smith's book, *Doctrines and Covenants* 93:29).

c. "What God was once, we are now; what God is now, we shall be" (*Manual of the Mormon Church,* Part I, p. 52).

We reply:

The Bible teaches very plainly that the *first* man Adam was created. To teach the pre-existence or co-existence of man is speculative and unscriptural. No self-conscious member of Adam's race can recollect or reflect upon his having existed in the beginning with God. Only God is before all things. To argue for man's pre-existence on the basis of such passages as Jer. 1:5 or verses dealing with God's sovereign election, is to discredit the wisdom, foreknowledge and omniscience of God.

Is it not blasphemy for Mormons to teach that God was once what we are now? To speak of an infinitely holy God as ever being like finite sinful men is sacrilege. This alone should persuade us that Mormonism is not Christian.

4. Concerning salvation, *they teach:*

a. The gospel of Jesus Christ is called the plan of salvation. It is a system of rules through which salvation may be gained. "We believe that the first principles and ordinances of the gospel are: first, Faith in the Lord Jesus Christ; second, Repentance; third, Baptism by immersion for the remission of sins; fourth, Laying on of hands for the gift of the Holy Ghost" (Fourth article of *The Articles of Faith of the Church of Jesus Christ of Latter-Day Saints).*

b. The saving ordinances of the church (baptism and laying on of hands) must be administered by men holding the priesthood, which is the authority of God delegated to men. "Without these divinely ordained and inspired men, holding this Holy Priesthood, the work of the ministry cannot be performed acceptably by God, neither can the church be perfected" (Taken from Charles W. Penrose's book, *Rays of Living Light,* p. 38).

c. Baptism is essential for salvation (James E. Talmage, *Articles of Faith,* p. 122). Baptism for the dead is also taught and practiced by the Mormons. Living Mormons are baptized by proxy for their dead ancestors who did not embrace the Mormon faith (Charles W. Penrose, *op. cit.,* p. 76).

d. They teach that salvation will be provided for the dead. Those who have not had opportunity to hear the message of the Mormons, when alive on earth, will be given a chance to repent after death.

"Since the days when the apostles and other authorized servants of Christ administered the ordinances of the gospel, and during the times when 'darkness covered the earth and gross darkness the people' down to the present age when it is claimed by the Latter-day Saints that the Church of Christ, the Holy Apostleship, and the fulness of the Gospel have been restored, myriads of good people have passed away without receiving the new birth in the manner that Christ declared to be essential. Have they all perished? Is it possible that they are doomed to destruction? Will the Eternal Father reject all these His children because they did not obey a law which was not made known to them?" (Charles W. Penrose, *op. cit.,* p. 69).

We reply:

Rom. 11:6
Eph. 2:8-9
Tit. 3:5
Acts 16:31
Matt. 1:21
John 1:12-13
Heb. 7:25
Acts 4:12

a. Salvation is by grace alone, not by works. It is not a *plan that saves us; it is a person. It is not a system* man needs; it is a Saviour. There are no saving ordinances. The ordinances are symbols of salvation but Christ alone can save.

John 3:16

b. It is proud presumption to declare that only the Mormon priesthood can administer the ordinances and salvation. Salvation is God's gift and it is available for any one who will come and take the water of life freely. Nowhere in the Word of God do we find that salvation must entail special ordinances conducted by men, specially ordained of God for that purpose. There is but one mediator between God and men, the man Christ Jesus. To assume that Mormon mediation is necessary for salvation is to assert that there were no saved people living on earth from the apostolic period to about the middle of the nineteenth century with the arrival of Joseph Smith.

Heb. 11

John 4:2

c. To say that baptism is essential for salvation is to assume that the saints of the Old Testament were not saved, that even Jesus did not save any one (since He personally baptized no one) that Zacchaeus was

Luke 19:1-10
Luke 23:43
Rom. 1:16
I Cor. 1:17
Acts 10:44
Rom. 8:9
Acts 2:4
Acts 10:44
Acts 8:14-17
Acts 19:6

Heb. 2:4
Gal. 4:6

Heb. 9:27
II Cor. 6:2
Acts 17:30

I Cor. 15

not saved, nor the thief on the cross. It is to declare that the apostle Paul did not preach a full gospel, nor practice it. Paul clearly distinguishes between the gospel and baptism when he says, "Christ sent me not to baptize, but to preach the gospel." The Holy Spirit fell upon the Gentile believers before they were baptized and "If any man have not the Spirit of Christ, he is none of His." Furthermore the Holy Spirit was received without the laying on of hands. The exceptions merely indicate the oneness of the Samaritan and Ephesian disciples with both the Jewish and the Gentile church. It is historical record, not doctrinal dictum. God is sovereign in the administration of the Spirit and His gifts and God implants the Spirit of His Son in the heart of all His sons.

d. The Bible does not teach that anyone will be given a chance to repent after death.

e. It is wrong to base belief in baptism for the dead on one obscure passage. It seems that Paul was showing the reasonableness of belief in the resurrection of the body by allusion to a heathen custom of "baptizing for the dead." The whole chapter is a polemic setting forth the certainty of the resurrection of the dead and he argues that belief in life after death is universally latent in human consciousness.

5. Concerning Jesus Christ, *they teach:*

a. "The fleshly body of Jesus required a mother as well as a father. Therefore the father and mother of Jesus according to the flesh must have been associated together as husband and wife; hence the virgin Mary must have been for the time being the lawful wife of God the Father" (*The Seer,* p. 159). "He was not begotten of the Holy Ghost" (*Journal of Discourses,* I, 50). Thus, Mormons deny the Virgin Birth of Christ.

b. "It was Jesus Christ who was married at Cana to the Marys and Martha, whereby He could see His seed before He was crucified" (Orson Hyde in his *Journal,* Vol. II, p. 80).

We reply:

a. To us, the Bible speaks plainly of the fact that Jesus Christ was virgin born, that the manner of His birth was prophesied in the Old Testament and fulfulled at His first Advent. Gen. 3:15; Isa. 7:14; 9:6; Jer. 31:22; Matt. 1:18-25; Luke 1:30-35; Gal. 4:4.

b. To speak of Jesus Christ as a polygamist, would be to concede that He violated His own teachings, was unworthy of respect and unfit to worship.

6. Concerning marriage, *they teach:*

a. "The Lord intended that the marriage covenant should be for time and eternity and the practice of marrying 'till death do us part' did not originate with the Lord, or his servants but is a man-made doctrine" (Le Grand Richard's book, *A Marvelous Work and a Wonder*, p. 163).

b. "The power to officiate in the ordinances of God has not been upon the earth since the great apostasy until the present century. Something like seventeen centuries have passed away since the authority was lost on the eastern hemisphere to administer in any of the ordinances of God. During that long period marriages have been celebrated according to the customs of human governments by uninspired men, holding no authority from God; consequently all their marriages, like their baptisms, are illegal before the Lord" (Orson Pratt, in *The Seer*, p. 48).

We reply:

a. They "do err, not knowing the scriptures, nor the power of God. For in the resurrection they neither marry nor are given in marriage, but are as the angels of God in heaven." Rom. 7:3 makes it clear that marriage is only for this life.

b. To say that all but Mormon marriages are illegal, is too ludicrous to even merit comment. Paul and the other apostles recognized marriage as binding no matter what authority united them in marriage. To disbelieve in the legal sanctity of even the marriage of an unbelieving husband to a believing wife, would be to sanction the birth of illegitimate children. Such a notion, Paul strongly denies. The children born to such an unequal union, are nevertheless "holy" that is, they are legitimate children. I Cor. 7:13-14.

Examination on Lesson XX

Marks	
5	1. How did Joseph Smith account for the origin of the Book of Mormon?
5	2. Tell us a few facts (at least 5) about Joseph Smith.
5	3. Tell us a few facts concerning his successor.
5	4. Give an explanation for the split that came to this movement.
5	5. On what Scripture do they base their belief for the union of the Bible with the Book of Mormon? What is your answer?
5	6. Give a few reasons for believing that the historical claims of Joseph Smith are without foundation.
5	7. How does the movement function? Where are its headquarters? What about its growth?
10	8. What do they teach about the Scriptures? Your reply?
10	9. What do they teach concerning God? Your reply?
10	10. What do they teach concerning man? Your reply?
5	11. What is the gospel according to the Mormons?
5	12. What do they teach about the administration of the ordinances?
5	13. What do they teach about baptism?
6	14. Locate four Scriptures to show that salvation is not by works.
10	15. Give *your* reasons for not accepting the mediation of a Mormon priesthood in the scheme of salvation.
10	16. Why do you not believe that baptism is essential for salvation?
5	17. Why do you consider it wrong to baptize for the dead?
6	18. What do they teach about Jesus Christ?
10	19. How do you reply to these claims?
10	20. What do they teach about marriage? Your reply?

$$\frac{137 \times 100}{137} = 100$$

Summary of Part III

The soul-winner must not deal haughtily or contemptuously with those ensnared by a cult. At the same time, he must not be weak or vacillating. He must be able to reprove and rebuke, but "with all longsuffering and doctrine." Controversy in the flesh will only strengthen the fetters that bind the deluded. The weapons of our warfare are not carnal: they are spiritual. Spiritual weapons alone are mighty through God to the pulling down of Satan's strongholds. The soul-winner who is endued with power from on high, who knows how to prevail at the throne of grace in prayer, who walks with God and is constrained by the love of Christ, can be the divine instrument for the emancipation of Satan's slaves, even those bound by the chains of a cult.

These last five lessons are preparatory in knowing how to deal with Cults. Sometimes there are stones to remove before Lazarus can be brought forth from the dead. With the stones of error removed, a simple word of gospel may bring a soul from death into life, from darkness into light. The salvation of a soul is a divine miracle and the simple gospel spoken by some trusting saint is still God's way of working such wonders.

BIBLIOGRAPHY

Biederwolf, William Edward. *Mormonism under the Searchlight.* Grand Rapids, Mich.: Wm. B. Eerdman's Publishing Co, 1954.

Basis for Belief in a New World. Brooklyn, New York: Watch Tower Bible and Tract Society, 1953.

Eddy, Mary Baker. *Science and Health with the Key to the Scriptures.* Norwood, Mass.: n.d.

Encyclopaedia Britannica. 14th ed. Vol. XV. Article, "Mormons."

———. 14th ed. Vol. XX. Article, "Joseph Smith."

———. 14th ed. Vol. XXIII. Article, "Brigham Young."

Haynes, Carlyle B. *Seventh-Day Adventists—Their Work and Teachings.* Oshawa, Canada: Canadian Watchman Press, 1935.

Jones, E. B. *40 Bible-Supported Reasons Why You Should Not Be a Seventh-Day Adventist,* Minneapolis, Minn.: Guardians of the Faith, 1949. 7th edition.

Let God Be True. Brooklyn, New York: Watch Tower Bible and Tract Society, n.d.

Martin, Walter R. and Klann, Norman H. *Jehovah of the Watchtower.* Martin and Klann. New York: Biblical Truth Publishing Society, 1953.

Penrose, Charles W. *Rays of Living Light.* This book of 80 pages is given out as free Mormon literature but has no indication of place, publisher or date.

Richards, Le Grand. *A Marvelous Work and a Wonder.* Salt Lake City, Utah: Deseret Book Co., 1950.

Russell, Charles Taze. *Studies in the Scriptures.* 6 Vols. Brooklyn, New York: Watch Tower Bible and Tract Society, 1897.

Rutherford, J. F. *The Harp of God*. Brooklyn, New York: International Bible Students Association, 1921.

————. *The Truth Shall Make You Free*. 300 Main St., Toronto, Canada: Jehovah's Witnesses of Canada, n.d.

Schwarz, Fred. *The Heart, Mind and Soul of Communism*. Waterloo, Iowa: Morris Printing Co., 1953.

————. *The Christian Answer to Communism*. Box 727, Anderson, Indiana: Great Commission Press, 1953.

————. *The Communist Interpretation of Peace*. Speech delivered by Dr. Schwarz in Congressional Dining Hall, Feb. 27, 1953. Waterloo, Iowa: Morris Printing Co., 1953.

Smith, Joseph. *The Doctrines and Covenants of the Church of Jesus Christ of the Latter-Day Saints*. Salt Lake City, Utah: published by The Church of Jesus Christ of Latter-Day Saints, 1952.

————. *Joseph Smith Tells His Own Story*. Salt Lake City, Utah: Deseret News Press, n.d.

Smith, Wilbur M. *The Bible and The World Today*. Scottdale, Pa.: Evangelical Fellowship, Inc., 1954.

Talmage, James E. *Articles of Faith*. Salt Lake City: published by The Church of Jesus Christ of Latter-Day Saints, 1950.

White, Ellen G. *The Great Controversy Between Christ and Satan*. Oshawa, Canada: Signs of the Times Publishing Association, 1944.